Cooking Club
Recipe Favorites 2012

A COMPILATION OF RECIPES AND TIPS FROM *COOKING CLUB* MAGAZINE

MINNETONKA, MINNESOTA

Cooking Club Recipe Favorites 2012

A Compilation of Recipes and Tips From *Cooking Club* magazine

Printed in 2011.

VICE PRESIDENT PRODUCT MARKETING
Laura Hunter

MANAGING EDITOR
Jen Weaverling

COVER DESIGN AND BOOK PRODUCTION
Jenny Mahoney

PHOTOGRAPHY
Stafford Photography

SPECIAL THANKS
Terry Casey, Jessica Doboszenski, Nicole Groessel and Betsy Wray

1 2 3 4 5 6 7 8 / 15 14 13 12 11
© 2011 Cooking Club of America
ISBN 978-1-58159-541-3

On the cover:
Creamy Chocolate-Malt Cake, page 124
On the back:
Meltingly Tender Pot Roast, page 68
Grilled Southwest Potato Salad, page 55
Cranberry-Raisin Bread with Cardamom, page 29

Cooking Club of America
12301 Whitewater Drive
Minnetonka, MN 55343
www.cookingclub.com

Contents

Cranberry-Raisin Bread with Cardamom, page 29

Tomatoes with Pesto and Asiago Cheese, page 51

Lamb Chops with Green Olive Tapenade, page 75

Cream Cheese-Apple Crisp, page 130

Cooking Club Recipe Favorites 2012

A COMPILATION OF RECIPES AND TIPS FROM *COOKING CLUB* MAGAZINE

For Cooking Club of America Members, culinary exploration is a way of life.

Sure, we all have our own specialty dishes that no one else in the world can make like us. But we're always up for new challenges, too. *Cooking Club Recipe Favorites 2012* presents everything you need to enhance your cooking skills and expand your recipe repertoire.

Here are 144 pages filled with best-of-the-best recipes from the award-winning pages of *Cooking Club* magazine. But that's not all. Good cooking is about culinary technique as well, so we've sprinkled this volume with tips and ideas to help take your skills to another level.

You're sure to find something for everybody and every occasion.

Delight guests with appetizers like Phyllo Triangles with Goat Cheese and Roasted Peppers. Bake wonderful breads, such as Cornmeal Muffins with Pan-Roasted Jalapeños and Cranberry-Raisin Bread with Cardamom. Make salads and sides everyone will love — creations like Grilled Southwest Potato Salad and Gorgonzola-Balsamic Greens with Pepper-Glazed Pecans.

You can never have enough main dish options, and recipes like Meltingly Tender Pot Roast and Lemon Chicken with Asparagus will get rave reviews. Of course, desserts top everything, and you'll be intrigued by the likes of Chocolate Angel Food Cake with Triple-Chocolate Glaze.

That's just a taste of what you'll find in the recipe-packed and picture-filled pages to come. Life's culinary exploration continues right here. We're very glad you're with us for the ride.

Spicy Two-Sausage Chili, page 98

Brownie Chunk Cheesecake, page 129

Citrus-Peppercorn-Spiked Tuna, page 87

Buttermilk-Parsley Mashed Potatoes with Bacon, page 39

Mixed Greens with Hazelnuts, Red Onion
and Goat Cheese, page 44

Mixed Berry Cobbler, page 132

Appetizers

Artichoke-Blue Cheese Crostini, page 9
Mozzarella-Tomato-Olive Cocktail Skewers, page 10

Artichoke-Blue Cheese Crostini

Crostini, thin slices of toasted bread topped with savory ingredients, make easy hand-held appetizers. The bread slices can be prepared in advance and stored in an airtight container or bag. If desired, crisp them briefly in a 400°F. oven for a few minutes before serving.

1   (8-oz.) baguette, cut diagonally into 24 slices (½ inch)
2   tablespoons extra-virgin olive oil
1   (14-oz.) can quartered artichoke hearts, well-drained
1   garlic clove, minced
½   cup (2 oz.) crumbled blue cheese
¼   cup chopped Kalamata olives
¼   cup sour cream or reduced-fat sour cream
2   tablespoons chopped fresh parsley
1   teaspoon lemon juice
⅛   teaspoon freshly ground pepper
1   tablespoon freshly grated Parmesan cheese

1 Heat broiler. Brush both sides of bread slices lightly with oil; place on baking sheet. Broil 4 to 6 inches from heat 4 to 6 minutes or until lightly browned, turning once. Cool. (Bread can be prepared up to 1 day ahead. Store in airtight container.)

2 Lightly brush 1½- to 2-cup gratin or baking dish with oil. Pat artichokes dry with paper towels; remove any tough or prickly bits. Place in food processor; pulse until chopped. Or chop by hand into ½-inch pieces. (You should have about 1 cup.)

3 In medium bowl, stir together artichokes, garlic, blue cheese, olives, sour cream, parsley, lemon juice and pepper. Spread mixture in baking dish; sprinkle with cheese. (Spread can be made to this point up to 1 day ahead. Cover and refrigerate.)

4 Heat oven to 375°F. Bake 20 to 30 minutes or until bubbly and lightly browned. Serve with toasted baguette slices.

24 crostini

PER CROSTINI: 55 calories, 3 g total fat (1 g saturated fat), 2 g protein, 6 g carbohydrate, 5 mg cholesterol, 130 mg sodium, .5 g fiber

RECIPE BY CAROLE BROWN

Mozzarella-Tomato-Olive Cocktail Skewers

These colorful skewers will liven up any appetizer buffet. They're simple to prepare but pack a lot of flavor. The skewers are especially delicious with very soft, fresh mozzarella cheese, which is available in some supermarkets and specialty cheese stores. Look for smaller balls labeled bocconcini (little mouthfuls) or ciliegini (small cherries).

4	oz. fresh mozzarella (small balls, if available)
16	grape tomatoes
16	pitted Kalamata olives
2	tablespoons extra-virgin olive oil
½	teaspoon minced garlic
¼	teaspoon dried thyme
⅛	teaspoon salt
⅛	teaspoon freshly ground black pepper
	Dash crushed red pepper
32	small fresh basil leaves plus additional for garnish, if desired
16	(4- to 6-inch) wooden skewers

1 Cut mozzarella into bite-sized pieces. If using small balls, keep whole. Place in medium bowl; stir in tomatoes, olives, oil, garlic, thyme, salt, black pepper and crushed red pepper. Cover and refrigerate 1 to 3 hours.

2 If basil leaves are large, cut into smaller pieces.

3 Thread marinated cheese, tomatoes and olives onto skewers, placing basil leaves in between. Place skewers on platter; garnish with additional fresh basil.

16 skewers

PER SKEWER: 45 calories, 4 g total fat (1.5 g saturated fat), 1.5 g protein, 1 g carbohydrate, 5 mg cholesterol, 90 mg sodium, .5 g fiber

RECIPE BY CAROLE BROWN

Olive-Pastry Spirals with Goat Cheese

Black olives provide the rich filling for these crispy little pastry bites. You can use either olive tapenade or olive paste; both are made from ground imported black olives, but tapenade also usually includes anchovies and additional flavorings. Look for them in the same aisle as the olives.

> 1 sheet frozen puff pastry (from 17.3-oz. pkg.), thawed
> 3 tablespoons Kalamata olive tapenade or olive paste
> 2 tablespoons thinly sliced green onions
> ¼ cup (1 oz.) soft goat cheese, room temperature
> 3 tablespoons thinly sliced fresh basil or 24 small leaves

1 Heat oven to 425°F. Line baking sheet with parchment paper.

2 Place puff pastry on work surface. Spread tapenade over surface of puff pastry, leaving about ½-inch border on two short ends; sprinkle with green onions. Starting at one of the short ends, roll up puff pastry; pinch seam to seal. Freeze 15 minutes. Slice into 24 pieces, turning roll to keep round when slicing. Place on baking sheet. (Spirals can be prepared to this point up to 1 day ahead. Cover and refrigerate.)

3 Bake 15 to 18 minutes or until golden brown and crisp. Top with goat cheese and basil; serve warm.

24 appetizers

PER APPETIZER: 60 calories, 4.5 g total fat (1.5 g saturated fat), 1.5 g protein,
4 g carbohydrate, 10 mg cholesterol, 45 mg sodium, 0 g fiber

Puff Pastry Tricks

Puff pastry filled with savory ingredients and rolled into logs makes delicious finger food for your guests. Olive-Pastry Spirals with Goat Cheese are easily assembled, but you must work quickly, keeping the dough cold as you go. Once the log is made, freeze it for 15 minutes before slicing. This makes it easier to cut. Use a sharp knife and saw gently back and forth. After cutting each slice, roll the log and gently reshape it into a round. If the log becomes too soft, simply refreeze it.

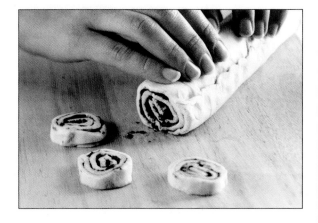

RECIPE BY MARY EVANS

Cambozola and Pear Skewers

Cambozola and Pear Skewers

Cambozola is a mild blue cheese from Germany. If you can't find it, substitute a fairly firm, not-too-ripe Brie or another mild blue cheese, such as Blue Castello.

    2 large firm but ripe Bartlett pears, peeled
    2 tablespoons butter
    1 tablespoon powdered sugar
   12 oz. Cambozola cheese

1 Cut each pear into 24 cubes.

2 Melt butter in large skillet over medium-high heat. Add pears; cook and stir 2 minutes or until browned and beginning to caramelize. Sprinkle with powdered sugar; cook 2 minutes or until lightly caramelized. Cool.

3 Meanwhile, cut cheese into 48 cubes. When pears are cool, skewer 1 pear cube and 1 cheese cube with 8-inch wooden skewers or toothpicks. Cover and refrigerate until ready to serve. Serve at room temperature.

48 appetizers

PER APPETIZER: 35 calories, 2.5 g total fat (1.5 g saturated fat), 1.5 g protein, 1.5 g carbohydrate, 10 mg cholesterol, 50 mg sodium, .5 g fiber

RECIPE BY MARY EVANS

Aged Cheddar
and Ale Fondue

Aged Cheddar and Ale Fondue

A take-off on beer-cheese soup, this hearty fondue pairs aged cheddar with your favorite microbrewed ale. Serve it with cubed rye bread on toothpicks or with vegetables.

2	tablespoons canola oil
1	tablespoon finely minced onion
3	tablespoons all-purpose flour
1¼	cups milk
⅓	cup ale or nonalcoholic beer
½	teaspoon celery salt
¼	teaspoon hot pepper sauce
1½	cups (6 oz.) shredded aged cheddar cheese
2	cups lightly packed cubed (1 inch) dark rye bread or 3 cups assorted fresh vegetables

1 Heat oil in medium saucepan over medium-low heat until hot. Add onion; cook 3 to 4 minutes or until softened, stirring frequently. Stir in flour; cook 1 minute, stirring frequently. Slowly whisk in milk and ale until smooth. Whisk in celery salt and hot pepper sauce. Increase heat to medium; bring to a boil. Boil 2 minutes or until slightly thickened, stirring constantly.

2 Remove from heat; slowly stir in cheese until melted. (Fondue can be prepared to this point up to 1 day ahead. Cover and refrigerate. Reheat gently over medium-low heat, stirring constantly.) Place in fondue pot on low heat or heat-proof ceramic pot or bowl over candle warmer. Serve with rye bread.

2 cups

PER 2 TABLESPOONS: 90 calories, 6 g total fat (2.5 g saturated fat), 4 g protein, 5 g carbohydrate, 15 mg cholesterol, 155 mg sodium, .5 g fiber

RECIPE BY MARY EVANS

Phyllo Triangles with Goat Cheese and Roasted Peppers

Crispy, bite-sized triangles of phyllo encase a distinctive medley of Mediterranean flavors. If you can't find pitted Kalamata olives, you can pit them yourself with a chef's knife. Simply press on the olive with the side of a knife blade to gently crush it and loosen the pit.

 4 oz. soft goat cheese
 ⅓ cup diced roasted red bell pepper (from 7-oz. jar), well-drained
 ¼ cup coarsely chopped pitted Kalamata olives
 ½ teaspoon dried oregano
 ⅛ teaspoon freshly ground pepper
 12 sheets frozen phyllo, thawed
 6 tablespoons melted butter, divided

1 Heat oven to 400°F. Line baking sheet with parchment paper. In medium bowl, stir together goat cheese, bell pepper, olives, oregano and pepper.

2 Unroll phyllo sheets; cover with dry towel. Place 1 phyllo sheet on work surface; cover with second sheet. Brush lightly with some of the melted butter. Cut into 4 (16×2½-inch) strips. Place 1 rounded teaspoon of the goat cheese mixture at bottom of each strip; fold like a flag up the length of the strip to form a triangle. Place on baking sheet. Repeat with remaining phyllo sheets.

3 Brush tops of appetizers with remaining butter. (Appetizers can be made to this point up to 1 day ahead. Cover and refrigerate.) Bake 12 to 14 minutes or until golden brown and crisp. Cool on wire rack 5 minutes.

24 appetizers

PER APPETIZER: 70 calories, 4 g total fat (2 g saturated fat), 2 g protein,
7 g carbohydrate, 10 mg cholesterol, 90 mg sodium, .5 g fiber

RECIPE BY MARY EVANS

Chipotle Meatballs

Because this appetizer uses purchased meatballs, it takes just a few minutes to prepare. The meatballs are bathed in a zesty sauce that gets smokiness and spice from chipotle chiles. For even more heat, add another chile or use a spicier salsa. The raspberry preserves lend a subtle sweetness.

- 1 (16-oz.) jar medium or mild chunky salsa
- 1 (12-oz.) jar seedless raspberry preserves
- 2 chipotle chiles in adobo sauce*
- 1 teaspoon adobo sauce
- ¾ teaspoon dried thyme
  Dash ground cloves
- 2 lb. fully cooked frozen meatballs, thawed
- 1 tablespoon chopped cilantro

1 Place salsa, preserves, chiles, adobo sauce, thyme and cloves in food processor or blender; process until smooth.

2 Place meatballs and chile mixture in Dutch oven. Bring just to a boil over medium heat. Reduce heat to low; cook 15 to 20 minutes or until meatballs are hot, stirring frequently. (Meatballs can be prepared to this point up to 1 day ahead. Cover and refrigerate. Reheat over medium-low heat until hot, stirring frequently.)

3 To serve, place in chafing dish or 4-quart slow cooker to keep warm; sprinkle with cilantro.

TIP *Chipotle chiles in adobo sauce can be found in the Hispanic foods section of most supermarkets. If desired, remove some or all of the seeds. Any remaining chipotle chiles can be covered and refrigerated about 1 week.

About 60 appetizers

PER APPETIZER: 60 calories, 2 g total fat (1 g saturated fat), 3 g protein, 7.5 g carbohydrate, 15 mg cholesterol, 135 mg sodium, .5 g fiber

RECIPE BY MARY EVANS

Shrimp with Bloody Mary Sauce

This snappy cocktail sauce is inspired by the Bloody Mary drink. The recipe is ideal for entertaining because both the shrimp and sauce can be prepared ahead of time. Although hot pepper sauce lends a bit of heat, it's not enough to overpower the other flavors.

SHRIMP

- 2½ **cups water**
- 2 **tablespoons white wine vinegar**
- 2 **(1-inch-wide) strips lemon peel***
- 1 **teaspoon salt**
- 1 **lb. shelled, deveined uncooked medium shrimp**

SAUCE

- 1 **(14.5-oz.) can diced tomatoes, well-drained**
- 1 **small garlic clove, minced**
- 1 **tablespoon lemon juice**
- 2 **teaspoons Worcestershire sauce**
- ¾ **teaspoon paprika**
- ¼ **teaspoon freshly ground pepper**
- ¼ **teaspoon hot pepper sauce**
- ⅛ **teaspoon celery seeds**
- ⅛ **teaspoon salt**
- 1 **tablespoon vodka, if desired**

1 In medium saucepan, combine water, vinegar, lemon peel and salt; bring to a gentle simmer over medium heat. Add shrimp; cook 3 to 6 minutes or until shrimp turn pink. Strain; spread shrimp on plate to cool. Cover and refrigerate until ready to serve.

2 Place all sauce ingredients except vodka in food processor or blender; process until sauce is almost smooth. Stir in vodka. Refrigerate at least 30 minutes. (Shrimp and sauce can be prepared up to 1 day ahead.) Serve shrimp with sauce.

TIP *Peel lemon with vegetable peeler.

6 servings

PER SERVING: 75 calories, .5 g total fat (0 g saturated fat), 12 g protein, 3.5 g carbohydrate, 110 mg cholesterol, 455 mg sodium, .5 g fiber

RECIPE BY CAROLE BROWN

Shrimp with Bloody Mary Sauce

Spicy Smoked Salmon Dip

Salmon can be either cold- or hot-smoked. Cold-smoking produces a silky texture (nova or lox are two examples). Hot-smoked salmon, often just labeled smoked salmon, looks like a firmer version of a salmon fillet; its more substantial texture is best in this recipe. For the prettiest dip, choose bright-pink fish.

6	oz. hot-smoked salmon*
½	cup mayonnaise
¼	cup plain yogurt
¼	cup plus 1 tablespoon sliced green onions, divided
1	teaspoon seafood seasoning, such as Old Bay
	Generous dash cayenne pepper or 1 teaspoon Asian chile sauce
6	cups assorted vegetables for dipping
	Bagel crisps or toasted pita wedges

1 Remove and discard skin and dark brown fatty layer from salmon. Break salmon into pieces. Pulse in food processor until finely chopped. Add mayonnaise, yogurt, ¼ cup of the green onions, seafood seasoning and cayenne pepper; pulse until blended.

2 Cover and refrigerate until ready to serve. Garnish with remaining 1 tablespoon green onion. Serve with vegetables and bagel crisps. (Dip can be made 1 day ahead.)

TIP *Look for hot-smoked salmon in the refrigerated section of the grocery store. If difficult to find, use shelf-stable smoked salmon.

1⅓ cups

PER 2 TABLESPOONS: 105 calories, 9.5 g total fat (1.5 g saturated fat), 3.5 g protein, 1 g carbohydrate, 10 mg cholesterol, 265 mg sodium, 0 g fiber

RECIPE BY MARY EVANS

Grilled Vegetables with Lemon-Basil Aioli Dipping Sauce

Lightly grilling the vegetables keeps them crisp enough to serve as crudités. Asparagus and red bell peppers make a lively color combination, but you can use various seasonal vegetables, such as broccoli, summer squash, mushrooms and other bell peppers.

AIOLI

- ⅔ cup mayonnaise
- ⅓ cup sour cream
- 2 tablespoons extra-virgin olive oil
- 1½ tablespoons lemon juice
- 3 tablespoons chopped fresh basil
- 2 tablespoons chopped fresh chives
- 1 tablespoon minced garlic
- 1 teaspoon grated lemon peel
- ½ teaspoon salt
- ½ teaspoon freshly ground pepper

VEGETABLES

- 1 lb. asparagus
- 2 large red bell peppers, cut into ½-inch strips
- 2 tablespoons extra-virgin olive oil
- ¼ teaspoon salt
- ¼ teaspoon freshly ground pepper

1 In small bowl, stir together mayonnaise, sour cream, 2 tablespoons oil and lemon juice. Stir in basil, chives, garlic, lemon peel, ½ teaspoon salt and ½ teaspoon pepper. Cover and refrigerate at least 30 minutes or up to 4 hours.

2 Heat grill. In large bowl, toss asparagus and bell peppers with 2 tablespoons oil, ¼ teaspoon salt and ¼ teaspoon pepper. Oil grill grates. Place vegetables on gas grill over medium-high heat or on charcoal grill 4 to 6 inches from medium-high coals. Cover grill; grill 3 to 5 minutes or until lightly charred and crisp-tender, turning once. (Vegetables can be made up to 2 hours ahead. Cover and store at room temperature.) Serve with aioli.

8 servings

PER SERVING: 240 calories, 23.5 g total fat (4.5 g saturated fat), 2.5 g protein, 7 g carbohydrate, 15 mg cholesterol, 335 mg sodium, 2 g fiber

RECIPE BY MELANIE BARNARD

Breads

Crunchy Whole Wheat Parmesan Bread, page 25
Spinach- and Feta-Stuffed Whole Wheat Baguettes, page 26
Raisin, Walnut and Cinnamon Whole Wheat Bread, page 27

Crunchy Whole Wheat Parmesan Bread

To make this pull-apart-style loaf, the dough is cut into squares but left intact before it's baked. Parmesan cheese sprinkled over the top provides a savory-salty note in every bite. Make the dough by hand, as instructed, or prepare it in a stand mixer with a paddle or dough hook.

BREAD

1¼	cups lukewarm water (85ºF. to 95ºF.)
1	(¼-oz.) pkg. active dry yeast (2¼ teaspoons)
1½	cups whole wheat flour
2	tablespoons olive oil
1½	teaspoons salt
1½	cups bread flour, divided
¼	cup (1 oz.) freshly shredded Parmesan cheese

TOPPING

1	egg white, beaten until foamy
1	tablespoon olive oil
½	cup (2 oz.) freshly shredded Parmesan cheese

1 Place water in large bowl; sprinkle with yeast. Let stand 30 seconds; stir until blended. Let stand 5 minutes or until yeast is foamy. Stir in whole wheat flour, 2 tablespoons oil and salt until batter is smooth. Slowly stir in 1 cup of the bread flour and ¼ cup cheese to form soft dough. (Dough will be sticky.) Cover; let stand 15 minutes.

2 Turn dough out onto lightly floured surface; knead 8 minutes or until dough is smooth and springy, using additional ½ cup bread flour as needed to keep dough from sticking.

3 Lightly oil clean large bowl. Place dough in bowl; turn to coat with oil. Cover; let rise in warm place 1 hour or until doubled in size. (Or cover and refrigerate at least 2 hours or up to 24 hours.)

4 Gently punch dough down; turn out onto lightly greased baking sheet. With greased hands, shape into 12-inch flat round loaf. Cover with clean towel; let rise in warm place 45 to 60 minutes or until loaf is almost doubled in size.

5 Meanwhile, place oven rack in lower third of oven. Heat oven to 375ºF. With sharp knife (dip knife in flour to avoid sticking), cut dough all the way through into 2-inch squares. (Leave loaf whole; do not separate into squares.) Lightly brush top with egg white.

6 Bake 35 minutes or until light brown on top and pale brown on bottom. Brush with 1 tablespoon oil; sprinkle with ½ cup cheese. Bake 5 minutes or until cheese is melted and bottom of bread is light brown. Remove from pan; cool completely on wire rack.

1 (32-piece) loaf

PER PIECE: 65 calories, 2 g total fat (.5 g saturated fat), 2.5 g protein, 9 g carbohydrate, 0 mg cholesterol, 155 mg sodium, 1 g fiber

RECIPE BY BEATRICE OJAKANGAS

Spinach- and Feta-Stuffed Whole Wheat Baguettes

Slicing into these baguettes reveals a swirl of spinach, herbs and cheese. Vinegar is added to give the loaves a bit of sourdough flavor. Reduce the heat as soon as the baguettes are placed in the oven to produce crusty bread without overbrowning.

BREAD

- 1½ **cups lukewarm water (85ºF. to 95ºF.)**
- 1 **(¼-oz.) pkg. active dry yeast (2¼ teaspoons)**
- 2 **tablespoons sugar**
- 2 **cups whole wheat flour**
- 1 **tablespoon white vinegar**
- 1 **teaspoon salt**
- 1½ **cups bread flour**

FILLING

- 2 **tablespoons butter or olive oil**
- ½ **cup finely chopped onion**
- 1 **garlic clove, minced**
- 1 **tablespoon finely chopped parsley**
- ½ **teaspoon salt**
- 2 **cups lightly packed fresh baby spinach**
- 1 **cup (4 oz.) crumbled feta cheese**

1 Place water in large bowl; sprinkle with yeast and sugar. Let stand 30 seconds; stir until blended. Let stand 5 minutes or until yeast is foamy. Stir in whole wheat flour, vinegar and 1 teaspoon salt until batter is smooth. Cover; let stand 15 minutes. Slowly stir in 1 cup of the bread flour to form soft dough. (Dough will be sticky.) Cover; let stand 15 minutes.

2 Turn dough out onto lightly floured surface; knead 5 to 10 minutes or until smooth and springy, using additional ½ cup bread flour as needed to keep dough from sticking.

3 Lightly oil clean large bowl. Place dough in bowl; turn to coat with oil. Cover; let rise in warm place 1 hour or until doubled in size. (Or cover and refrigerate at least 2 hours or up to 24 hours.)

4 Meanwhile, melt butter in small skillet over medium heat. Add onion and garlic; cook 2 to 3 minutes or until soft. Remove from heat; stir in parsley and ½ teaspoon salt.

5 Lightly grease baking sheet or line with parchment paper. Turn dough out onto floured surface; divide in half. Pat or roll each half into 12-inch square. Spread each square with half of the onion mixture; layer with half of the spinach. Sprinkle each with half of the cheese.

6 Tightly roll each dough square into log, enclosing filling. Pinch edges to seal. Place loaves, seam sides down, on baking sheet. Cover with clean towel; let rise in warm place 45 minutes or until doubled in size.

7 Meanwhile, heat oven to 500ºF. Spray loaves with water. With sharp knife, make 4 (¼-inch-deep) diagonal cuts in top of each loaf. Place bread in oven; immediately reduce oven temperature to 400ºF. Bake 20 to 25 minutes or until lightly browned and bottoms of loaves sound hollow when gently tapped. Remove from pan; cool completely on wire rack.

2 (20-slice) loaves

PER SLICE: 60 calories, 1.5 g total fat (1 g saturated fat), 2 g protein, 9.5 g carbohydrate, 5 mg cholesterol, 135 mg sodium, 1 g fiber

RECIPE BY BEATRICE OJAKANGAS

Raisin, Walnut and Cinnamon Whole Wheat Bread

The sweetness of raisins and the crunch of walnuts add dimension to these loaves, while cinnamon and honey bring out the flavor of the whole wheat. It's the perfect bread for toasting.

½ cup warm water (85°F. to 95°F.)
1 (¼-oz.) pkg. active dry yeast (2¼ teaspoons)
1½ cups lukewarm whole milk (85°F. to 95°F.)
¼ cup honey
3 tablespoons unsalted butter, melted, divided
2 cups whole wheat flour
2 teaspoons ground cinnamon
2 teaspoons salt
2½ to 3 cups bread flour, divided
¾ cup raisins
¾ cup chopped walnuts

1 Place water in large bowl; sprinkle with yeast. Let stand 30 seconds; stir until blended. Let stand 5 minutes or until yeast is foamy. Stir in milk, honey and 2 tablespoons of the butter. Stir in whole wheat flour, cinnamon and salt until batter is smooth. Slowly stir in 1 cup of the bread flour, raisins and walnuts. Cover; let stand 15 minutes.

2 Stir in enough of the remaining bread flour to form soft dough. (Dough will be sticky.) Turn dough out onto lightly floured surface; knead 8 to 10 minutes or until dough is smooth and springy, using remaining bread flour as needed to keep dough from sticking.

3 Lightly oil clean large bowl. Place dough in bowl; turn to coat with oil. Cover; let rise in warm place 1 hour or until doubled in size.

4 Spray 2 (8¼×4½-inch) loaf pans with nonstick cooking spray. Punch dough down. Turn out onto lightly floured surface; divide in half. Shape each half into oblong loaf; place in pans. Cover; let rise in warm place 45 to 60 minutes or until doubled in size.

5 Meanwhile, heat oven to 350°F. Bake 45 to 50 minutes or until bottoms of loaves sound hollow when removed from pan and gently tapped. Brush tops with remaining 1 tablespoon butter. Cool in pans 15 minutes; remove bread from pans. Cool completely on wire rack.

2 (14-slice) loaves

PER SLICE: 135 calories, 4 g total fat (1.5 g saturated fat), 3.5 g protein, 22.5 g carbohydrate, 5 mg cholesterol, 175 mg sodium, 2 g fiber

Whole Wheat Guide

Gluten is responsible for the lightness and texture of a loaf. Whole wheat flour has less gluten than white flour, resulting in a denser loaf. Bread made entirely of whole wheat can be too dense, however. To make these recipes lighter, they contain about 50 percent whole wheat flour.

Kneading Tips

Whole wheat bread dough is stickier than white flour dough, so it requires a somewhat different approach:

- Lightly oil your hands, and spray the surface with non-stick cooking spray.

- Be careful how much flour you add. Too much produces a dry, heavy loaf that will not rise easily. When the dough has sufficient flour added, it should be slightly sticky and hold its shape rather than slump.

- Handle the dough gently and turn it frequently as you knead it.

RECIPE BY BEATRICE OJAKANGAS

Cranberry-Raisin Bread with Cardamom

Cranberry-Raisin Bread with Cardamom

Life member David Heppner has been baking bread for more than two decades. And for the past few years, he's been playing with recipes and creating his own. "I love working in the kitchen, fooling around with and changing recipes to suit me," he says. David added the cardamom on his second—and final—try of this one; it's the perfect partner for the cranberries.

6	cups bread flour
½	cup nonfat dry milk
¼	cup packed light brown sugar
¼	cup wheat gluten*
2	(¼-oz.) pkg. rapid rise yeast
1	tablespoon ground cardamom
2	teaspoons salt
1⅓	cups golden raisins
1⅓	cups dried cranberries
2½	cups water
¼	cup unsalted butter, cut up
1	egg, beaten
1	tablespoon water

1 Generously grease 2 (9×5-inch) loaf pans with shortening. In large bowl, stir together flour, dry milk, brown sugar, wheat gluten, yeast, cardamom, salt, raisins and cranberries.

2 Place water and butter in medium saucepan; heat over low heat until butter is melted and mixture reaches 120°F. to 130°F. Pour hot butter mixture into flour mixture. Using mixer with dough hook, mix at medium speed 5 to 7 minutes or until soft and smooth. (Or mix by hand until dough forms. On lightly floured surface, knead dough until soft and smooth, about 10 minutes.) Cover and let stand 10 minutes.

3 Turn dough out onto lightly floured surface; knead briefly. Divide in half. Roll each half into 8-inch log; place in pans. Let rise 30 minutes or until doubled in size.

4 Meanwhile, heat oven to 350°F. In small bowl, whisk together egg and water. Lightly brush tops of loaves with egg mixture. With sharp knife, make 3 to 4 slashes in tops of loaves. Bake 30 to 35 minutes or until golden brown and bottoms of loaves sound hollow when tapped.

TIP *Wheat gluten, also called vital wheat gluten, improves the texture of and promotes rising in hearty yeast breads. Look for it in the baking section of the grocery store or order it from www.kingarthurflour.com.

2 (16-slice) loaves

PER SLICE: 165 calories, 2 g total fat (1 g saturated fat), 6 g protein, 31.5 g carbohydrate, 10 mg cholesterol, 160 mg sodium, 1.5 g fiber

RECIPE BY LIFE MEMBER DAVID HEPPNER, BRANDON, FL

Cornmeal Muffins with Pan-Roasted Jalapeños

Deliciously rich and buttery, these muffins are well-suited for serving with savory chili because they're not overly sweet. For an even better texture and more corn flavor, make them with stone-ground cornmeal.

- 1 teaspoon vegetable oil
- 2 jalapeño chiles, seeded, deveined
- 1¼ cups yellow cornmeal
- ¾ cup all-purpose flour
- 2 tablespoons sugar
- 1½ teaspoons baking powder
- ½ teaspoon baking soda
- ½ teaspoon salt
- 2 eggs, beaten
- 1 cup buttermilk
- ½ cup sour cream
- ¼ cup unsalted butter, melted

1 Heat oil in small skillet over medium heat until hot. Add chiles; cook and stir 2 minutes or until softened and beginning to brown. Remove chiles; cool. Finely chop.

2 Heat oven to 400°F. Grease bottoms of 12 muffin cups or line with paper liners. Whisk cornmeal, flour, sugar, baking powder, baking soda and salt in medium bowl until well-blended. Combine all remaining ingredients in large bowl. Stir cornmeal mixture into buttermilk mixture just until dry ingredients are moistened. Gently stir in chiles.

3 Spoon batter into muffin cups. Bake 15 to 18 minutes or until toothpick inserted in center comes out clean. Cool on wire rack 10 minutes; remove from pan. Serve warm or at room temperature.

12 muffins

PER MUFFIN: 165 calories, 7.5 g total fat (4 g saturated fat), 4 g protein,
21 g carbohydrate, 55 mg cholesterol, 250 mg sodium, 1 g fiber

RECIPE BY JILL VAN CLEAVE

Black Pepper Biscuits

Baking powder biscuits are as Southern as you can get. Flaky and tender, they're at their best served warm or shortly after emerging from a hot oven. This version is spiced up with the addition of lots of cracked pepper.

> 3 **cups all-purpose flour**
> 4 **teaspoons sugar**
> 4 **teaspoons baking powder**
> 2 **teaspoons cracked black pepper***
> 1 **teaspoon salt**
> ½ **cup plus 2 tablespoons unsalted butter, chilled, cut up, divided**
> 1 **cup cold whole milk**

1 Heat oven to 425°F. Line two baking sheets with parchment paper. In large bowl, whisk together flour, sugar, baking powder, pepper and salt. With pastry blender or 2 knives, cut in ½ cup of the butter until mixture resembles coarse crumbs with some pea-sized pieces. Stir in milk just until soft dough forms.

2 On lightly floured surface, pat or gently roll out dough to ¾-inch thickness. With floured biscuit cutter, cut into 2-inch rounds, pushing straight down and pulling up without twisting cutter. Place on baking sheets. Press scraps together to use all the dough.

3 Melt remaining 2 tablespoons butter; brush over tops of biscuits. Bake 10 to 12 minutes or until light golden brown on tops and golden brown on bottoms. Cool briefly on wire rack.

TIP *Cracked black pepper can be purchased in the spice aisle of the grocery store. To crack your own, place whole peppercorns in heavy resealable plastic bag; seal bag. Pound with flat side of meat mallet until coarsely chopped.

18 biscuits

PER BISCUIT: 155 calories, 7.5 g total fat (4.5 g saturated fat), 3 g protein, 18.5 g carbohydrate, 20 mg cholesterol, 250 mg sodium, .5 g fiber

RECIPE BY JILL VAN CLEAVE

Apricot-Almond Muffins

Chewy bits of dried apricots and crunchy slices of almonds fill these muffins with taste, texture and flashes of orange color. Make sure the dried apricots are still soft and pliable, and use pure almond extract, not the imitation variety, for best flavor.

MUFFINS

- ¾ cup diced dried apricots
- 1 tablespoon hot water
- 1 tablespoon lemon juice
- 1¾ cups all-purpose flour
- ½ cup sugar
- 1 teaspoon baking powder
- ½ teaspoon baking soda
- ¼ teaspoon salt
- 6 tablespoons unsalted butter, melted, cooled to room temperature
- 1 egg
- 1 (6-oz.) carton low-fat custard-style vanilla yogurt
- ¼ cup apricot preserves
- ¾ teaspoon almond extract
- ½ cup sliced almonds

GLAZE

- ¼ cup powdered sugar
- 1 teaspoon milk
- ½ teaspoon almond extract

1 Heat oven to 400°F. Grease bottoms of 12 muffin cups or line with paper liners. In small bowl, stir together apricots, water and lemon juice; let stand 10 minutes.

2 In large bowl, whisk together flour, sugar, baking powder, baking soda and salt. Make well in center. In medium bowl, whisk butter and egg until well-blended; whisk in yogurt until combined. Whisk in preserves and ¾ teaspoon almond extract. Pour mixture into well in center of flour mixture; stir until partially mixed. Add apricots; stir until just blended.

3 Divide evenly among muffin cups; sprinkle with sliced almonds. Bake 20 to 25 minutes or until golden brown and toothpick inserted in center comes out clean. Cool in pan on wire rack 10 minutes.

4 Meanwhile, in another small bowl, stir together all glaze ingredients. Drizzle over muffins; remove from pan. Serve warm or at room temperature.

Tips

Why grease only the bottom?
If you're not using paper liners, it's important to grease the bottoms of muffin cups so the muffins release easily after baking. But the muffins will rise better and more evenly during baking if you don't grease the sides. The batter can then cling to the sides as it rises. Grease the bottoms with shortening, applied with waxed paper or a paper towel, or spray with nonstick cooking spray.

Why cool muffins in the pan?
Right after taking them out of the oven, muffins should cool for a short time—about 10 minutes—in the pan on a rack. If they're removed from the pan right away, they may break apart because they're fragile when hot. In addition, if the muffins are baked without liners, the cooling time gives them a chance to release slightly from the sides of the pan. Don't let them cool too long in the pan, however, or they won't release as easily.

12 muffins

PER MUFFIN: 245 calories, 8.5 g total fat (4 g saturated fat), 4 g protein, 38 g carbohydrate, 35 mg cholesterol, 160 mg sodium, 1.5 g fiber

RECIPE BY MARY EVANS

Apricot-Almond Muffins

Lemon Cream Scones

These delicate, buttery scones are extremely tender. The key to keeping them that way is to handle the dough as little as possible. Take a cue from the British and serve them with Lemon Cream, a tangy whipped cream reminiscent of clotted cream from Cornwall; or top them with a sweet raspberry jam.

2¼	cups all-purpose flour
⅓	cup plus 2 teaspoons sugar, divided
1	tablespoon baking powder
¼	teaspoon salt
½	cup unsalted butter, chilled, cut up
¾	cup plus 1 tablespoon whipping cream, divided
2	egg yolks
1	tablespoon grated lemon peel
	Lemon Cream (recipe follows)

1 Heat oven to 400°F. Line baking sheet with parchment paper. In large bowl, whisk together flour, ⅓ cup of the sugar, baking powder and salt. With pastry blender or 2 knives, cut in butter until butter is size of blueberries.

2 In small bowl, whisk together ¾ cup of the cream, egg yolks and lemon peel. Pour into flour mixture; stir with fork until evenly moistened. With hands, quickly and gently press together to form dough. On lightly floured surface, pat into 7-inch round 1 inch thick. With 2½-inch round cutter, cut into 8 rounds, pressing together dough scraps as necessary. Place on baking sheet.

3 Lightly brush top of scones with remaining 1 tablespoon cream; sprinkle with remaining 2 teaspoons sugar. Bake 15 to 18 minutes or until toothpick inserted in center comes out clean. Cool on wire rack 10 minutes. Serve warm or at room temperature with Lemon Cream.

8 scones

PER SCONE: 430 calories, 28 g total fat (17 g saturated fat), 5.5 g protein, 40 g carbohydrate, 135 mg cholesterol, 280 mg sodium, 1 g fiber

Lemon Cream

½	cup whipping cream
1	tablespoon sugar
½	cup sour cream
1	teaspoon grated lemon peel

In medium bowl, beat whipping cream and sugar at medium-high speed until soft peaks form. Fold in sour cream and lemon peel.

RECIPES BY JANICE COLE

Easy Steps to Tender Scones

For the lightest, most delicate scones, follow these tips and serve them fresh from the oven.

- Use chilled butter and blend it into the flour mixture using a pastry blender or two knives. (If your hands tend to be cold, you can use your hands, as some pastry chefs do. Otherwise, use tools so the butter doesn't melt.)

- Work the butter into the flour mixture until it's about the size of blueberries. As the scones bake, the butter slowly melts, creating pockets of air that make the scones flaky, light and tender.

- Use a fork to blend the liquid with the dry ingredients. Work quickly so that the dough will be soft, with little gluten. The more you mix the dough, the more gluten will develop, resulting in tougher scones.

- It's not necessary to knead this dough. Just quickly and gently press the dough with your hands until it holds together. To avoid developing gluten strands, which make the dough tough, don't overwork it or squeeze it.

- Pat the dough into a 1-inch-thick round, working on parchment paper for wedges or on a lightly floured surface for cutouts. Make sure the dough remains thick; if it's too thin, the scones will be drier inside.

- For wedges, cut the round into 8 pieces and separate the wedges slightly before baking. They'll come back together during baking, but they'll be easier to cut apart. For cutouts, leave enough room between the scones so they won't bake together and will have crisp edges.

- For a pretty finish, brush the tops of the scones with an egg wash (egg mixed with water) or cream, and sprinkle them with sugar. For a sparkly effect, use large crystallized sugar.

Blend cold butter into the flour mixture until the butter particles are blueberry-sized.

Add the liquid to the dry ingredients; then use a fork to evenly distribute the moisture.

Gently press the dough together with your hands, taking care not to overwork it.

Pat out the dough to 1-inch thickness before cutting it into wedges or making cutouts. Don't pat it too thin or the scones will be dry.

Slightly separate wedges on parchment paper to allow for expansion during baking. They'll be easier to cut when done.

Salads & Sides

Buttermilk-Parsley
Mashed Potatoes with Bacon

Buttermilk-Parsley Mashed Potatoes with Bacon

This side dish is a completely new take on traditional mashed potatoes. It's based on the Irish peasant dish colcannon, which is a baked mixture of mashed potatoes and cabbage. In this version, parsley is sautéed with bacon, replacing the cabbage and adding marvelous herb flavor. There's no need to remove all the stems from the parsley; just wash the bunches, cut off most of the stems and pull out any very large stems before chopping.

2½	lb. Yukon Gold potatoes, peeled, cut into 2-inch pieces
1	tablespoon plus 1 teaspoon kosher (coarse) salt, divided
2	teaspoons vegetable oil
4	oz. bacon, diced
2	cups lightly packed very coarsely chopped fresh parsley
½	cup hot water
1	cup chopped green onions
¾	cup buttermilk
¼	cup unsalted butter
¼	teaspoon freshly ground pepper

1 Heat oven to 375°F. Butter shallow 2- to 3-quart glass or ceramic baking dish.

2 Place potatoes in large pot with enough cold water to cover; add 1 tablespoon of the salt. Bring to a boil over medium-high heat; boil 15 minutes or until tender. Drain. Reserve pot.

3 Meanwhile, heat oil in large skillet over medium heat until hot. Add bacon; cook until nearly crisp, stirring frequently. Pour off half of the drippings. Add parsley and hot water; cook 5 minutes or until liquid evaporates and parsley is tender. Add green onions; cook 30 seconds.

4 Place buttermilk, butter, remaining 1 teaspoon salt and pepper in same pot used to cook potatoes; bring to a simmer over medium heat. (Buttermilk will look curdled). Add potatoes; mash with potato masher. Stir in parsley mixture.

5 Spread potatoes in baking dish, leaving top uneven so potato peaks brown. (Potatoes can be prepared to this point up to 1 day ahead. Cover and refrigerate. Increase baking time 10 to 15 minutes.) Bake 30 minutes or until browned on edges and peaks.

8 (¾-cup) servings

PER SERVING: 230 calories, 11 g total fat (5.5 g saturated fat), 3 g protein, 28.5 g carbohydrate, 20 mg cholesterol, 740 mg sodium, 3.5 g fiber

RECIPE BY JERRY TRAUNFELD

Two-Potato Kugel

Kugel is a baked pudding that's served as a side dish. It can take on many forms, from a savory, dense potato and onion cake to a rich, sweet egg noodle casserole studded with raisins. This one, slightly sweet from sweet potatoes and currants, falls somewhere in between those two styles. Dill adds a spark of flavor that makes the recipe fresh and intriguing. The kugel is an ideal match for turkey.

¼ cup unsalted butter

1 large onion, finely chopped

2 lb. russet potatoes (about 3 large), peeled

1½ lb. sweet potatoes (1 to 2 large), peeled*

1 (8-oz.) pkg. cream cheese, softened

6 eggs

1 cup sour cream

1 tablespoon kosher (coarse) salt

1½ cups dried currants or raisins

½ cup chopped fresh dill

1 Heat oven to 350°F. Butter 13×9-inch glass or ceramic baking dish.

2 Melt butter in medium skillet over medium heat. Add onion; cook 5 minutes or until softened but not browned. With medium holes of box grater or shredding disk of food processor, grate potatoes; squeeze out extra moisture. Grate sweet potatoes.

3 In large bowl, beat cream cheese at medium speed until smooth. Beat in eggs one at a time. Beat in sour cream and salt. Stir in onion, potatoes, sweet potatoes, currants and dill. Spread evenly in baking dish. (Kugel can be made to this point up to 2 hours ahead. Cover and refrigerate.) Bake 55 to 60 minutes or until edges are browned and middle is firm. Cut into squares; serve warm.

TIP *Look for deep orange-colored sweet potatoes, often labeled as yams.

12 servings

PER SERVING: 320 calories, 17 g total fat (9.5 g saturated fat), 8 g protein, 37 g carbohydrate, 150 mg cholesterol, 505 mg sodium, 4 g fiber

RECIPE BY JERRY TRAUNFELD

Asiago Smashed Potatoes

Life member Kerry McGuire-Corum hates lumpy, gravy-laden mashed potatoes. One day, she decided to create a better version with red potatoes and ingredients from her fridge that needed to be used up. "These potatoes are so yummy," Kerry says, "you won't ever want anything else!"

4	lb. red potatoes, unpeeled, quartered
1½	teaspoons salt, divided
10	oz. Asiago cheese, shredded*
½	cup butter, cut up
½	cup milk
½	cup sour cream
½	cup sliced green onions
½	cup crumbled cooked bacon
¼	teaspoon freshly ground pepper

1 Place potatoes in large saucepan or Dutch oven; add enough water to cover. Stir in 1 teaspoon of the salt. Bring to a boil over medium-high heat. Reduce heat to medium; boil 20 to 30 minutes or until potatoes are tender when pierced with knife. Drain well.

2 Return potatoes to pan. Add all remaining ingredients, including remaining ½ teaspoon salt. Mash potatoes with potato masher.

TIP *Asiago cheese is made from cow's milk and has a firm texture and a nutty flavor. It's similar to Parmesan cheese and can be grated or shredded.

14 (about ¾-cup) servings

PER SERVING: 275 calories, 15 g total fat (8 g saturated fat), 11 g protein, 24.5 g carbohydrate, 40 mg cholesterol, 825 mg sodium, 3 g fiber

RECIPE BY LIFE MEMBER KERRY MCGUIRE-CORUM, GRANADA HILLS, CA

Butternut Squash with Walnut Crumb Topping, page 43
Mixed Greens with Hazelnuts, Red Onion and Goat Cheese, page 44

Butternut Squash with Walnut Crumb Topping

A take-off on the colonial dessert called brown betty, this recipe layers squash, onions, apples and buttered bread crumbs for a marvelous side dish. The walnuts provide a satisfying crunch.

- 1 cup unseasoned dry bread crumbs
- ½ cup finely chopped walnuts
- 1 teaspoon dried sage
- 1 teaspoon salt, divided
- ¼ teaspoon white pepper, divided
- Dash nutmeg
- ¼ cup butter, melted
- 1¼ lb. butternut squash, peeled, halved lengthwise, sliced (⅛ inch) (about 3 cups)
- 1 large Granny Smith apple, peeled, halved lengthwise, thinly sliced
- 1 medium onion, halved, thinly sliced
- 2 tablespoons canola oil

1 Heat oven to 425°F. Spray 9-inch deep-dish pie pan or 2-quart glass or ceramic baking dish with nonstick cooking spray.

2 In medium bowl, stir together bread crumbs, walnuts, sage, ½ teaspoon of the salt, ⅛ teaspoon of the pepper and nutmeg. Add melted butter; stir with fork to blend well. Sprinkle half of the crumb mixture over bottom of pan.

3 In large bowl, toss squash, apple, onion, remaining ½ teaspoon salt and remaining ⅛ teaspoon pepper with oil to coat; spread over crumbs in pan. Top with remaining crumb mixture. Cover pan tightly with foil; bake 40 minutes or until squash is just tender. Remove foil; reduce oven temperature to 350°F. Bake an additional 15 to 20 minutes or until crumbs are well-browned and squash is fork-tender.

8 servings

PER SERVING: 220 calories, 15 g total fat (4 g saturated fat), 3.5 g protein, 20.5 g carbohydrate, 15 mg cholesterol, 450 mg sodium, 2 g fiber

RECIPE BY MARY EVANS

Mixed Greens with Hazelnuts, Red Onion and Goat Cheese

Creamy goat cheese and crunchy hazelnuts grace a salad that's simple yet elegant. The mustard-spiked vinaigrette is a perfectly delicious complement to the mixed greens.

VINAIGRETTE

2	tablespoons heavy whipping cream
1	tablespoon Dijon mustard
1	tablespoon tarragon vinegar
¼	teaspoon salt
⅛	teaspoon freshly ground pepper
⅓	cup canola oil
2	tablespoons minced shallots

SALAD

2	thin slices red onion, halved
9	cups mixed salad greens
6	oz. soft goat cheese, crumbled
¾	cup toasted skinned hazelnuts, coarsely chopped*

1 In small bowl, whisk together cream, mustard, vinegar, salt and pepper. Whisk in oil; stir in shallots.

2 Soak onion slices in small bowl of ice water 15 minutes. Drain; pat dry.

3 To serve, toss greens in large bowl with enough vinaigrette to lightly coat; divide among 8 salad plates. Arrange onion slices over greens; sprinkle with cheese and hazelnuts.

TIP *To skin hazelnuts, place nuts on baking sheet. Bake at 375°F. for 4 to 6 minutes or until slightly darker in color and skins begin to crack. Place on kitchen towel; cool slightly. Briskly rub hazelnuts with towel until skins flake off. Some stubborn skins may remain, which is okay.

8 (1-cup) servings

PER SERVING: 240 calories, 23 g total fat (5 g saturated fat), 7 g protein, 5 g carbohydrate, 15 mg cholesterol, 215 mg sodium, 2.5 g fiber

RECIPE BY MARY EVANS

Lemon-Garlic Vegetables

The lemon flavor in this dish is unbelievable! It brightens a rather simple pairing of vegetables, while letting their fresh flavors shine through. Try the lemon-garlic butter on salmon, too.

- 1 lemon
- 5 tablespoons butter
- 1 tablespoon chopped garlic
- 1½ cups baby carrots
- 1½ cups red pearl onions, peeled*
- 1½ cups cauliflower florets
- 1½ cups broccoli florets
- ½ teaspoon salt
- ⅛ teaspoon freshly ground pepper

1 With vegetable peeler, remove outer layer of peel from lemon, avoiding bitter white pith beneath peel; place peel in small saucepan. Add butter and garlic. Heat over low heat until butter is melted; simmer 5 minutes. (Do not brown butter or garlic; remove from heat occasionally if necessary.) Remove from heat; let stand 15 minutes. Strain; discard lemon peel and garlic. Skim off any foam or particles from surface; let remaining particles settle to bottom. Pour off clear butter, leaving milky residue on bottom. Cover and refrigerate until ready to serve. (Butter can be prepared up to 3 days ahead.)

2 Fill large saucepan half full with water; bring to a boil over medium heat. Add carrots; boil 5 minutes. Add peeled onions; boil 3 minutes. Add cauliflower and broccoli; boil 3 minutes or until vegetables are crisp-tender. Drain thoroughly. Run cold water over vegetables to stop cooking; drain well. (Vegetables can be prepared to this point up to 1 day ahead. Cover and refrigerate.)

3 To serve, melt lemon-garlic butter in large skillet over medium heat. Add vegetables; cook 1 to 2 minutes or until heated through. (If vegetables have been refrigerated, cook 5 minutes or until heated through.) Sprinkle with salt and pepper.

TIP *To peel pearl onions, place in boiling water and boil 3 minutes. Drain; rinse with cold water to cool. Cut off root end and squeeze opposite end (onion should pop right out of its skin).

6 (scant 1-cup) servings

PER SERVING: 105 calories, 8 g total fat (5 g saturated fat), 2 g protein, 8 g carbohydrate, 20 mg cholesterol, 220 mg sodium, 2.5 g fiber

RECIPE BY MARY EVANS

Roasted Cauliflower with Red Pepper Butter, page 47
Steamed Broccoli with Fennel-Garlic Dressing, page 48

Roasted Cauliflower with Red Pepper Butter

Roasting intensifies and sweetens cauliflower's natural flavor in this appealing dish. A butter flavored with roasted red bell pepper lends richness, while bread crumbs provide a delicious toasted taste and texture.

¼ cup unsalted butter, melted

2 tablespoons finely chopped purchased roasted red bell pepper (pat dry before chopping)

¾ teaspoon paprika

¼ teaspoon salt

⅛ teaspoon freshly ground pepper

1 (1¾-lb.) head cauliflower, cut into florets (about 6 cups)

¼ cup unseasoned dry bread crumbs

1 In small bowl, stir together butter and bell pepper. Stir in paprika, salt and pepper until well-blended. (Mixture can be prepared up to 3 days ahead. Cover and refrigerate. Melt butter before using.)

2 Cook cauliflower in large pot of boiling salted water 1 to 3 minutes or until almost crisp-tender. Rinse under cold running water; drain well. In large bowl, toss cauliflower with red pepper butter. Add bread crumbs; toss to coat. (Cauliflower can be prepared to this point up to 2 hours ahead. Cover and refrigerate.)

3 Heat oven to 425°F. Place cauliflower on small rimmed baking sheet; bake 15 minutes or until hot and tender. Stir before serving.

8 (¾-cup) servings

PER SERVING: 85 calories, 6 g total fat (3.5 g saturated fat), 2 g protein, 6.5 g carbohydrate, 15 mg cholesterol, 120 mg sodium, 2 g fiber

RECIPE BY JILL VAN CLEAVE

Steamed Broccoli with Fennel-Garlic Dressing

Perk up a traditional broccoli side dish with a lemony vinaigrette that's subtly seasoned with toasted fennel seeds and crushed red pepper. While the recipe calls for using just broccoli florets, you can peel and slice the stems and add them as well.

½	teaspoon fennel seeds
1	garlic clove, minced
1	tablespoon lemon juice
¼	teaspoon salt
⅛	teaspoon crushed red pepper
3	tablespoons extra-virgin olive oil
1¼	lb. broccoli florets (about 8 cups)

1 Place fennel seeds in small dry skillet; toast over medium heat 2 to 3 minutes or until fragrant, stirring frequently. Crush with mortar and pestle or grind in spice grinder.

2 In small bowl, stir together ground fennel seeds, garlic, lemon juice, salt and crushed red pepper. Whisk in oil until well-blended. (Dressing can be made up to 2 days ahead. Cover and refrigerate.)

3 Place broccoli in steamer basket over boiling water. Cover and steam 5 minutes or until crisp-tender. In large bowl, toss broccoli with enough dressing to lightly coat. Serve warm.

8 (¾-cup) servings

PER SERVING: 70 calories, 5.5 g total fat (.5 g saturated fat), 2 g protein, 5 g carbohydrate, 0 mg cholesterol, 100 mg sodium, 2 g fiber

RECIPE BY JILL VAN CLEAVE

Tossed Orange-Walnut Salad with Balsamic Dressing

This leafy green salad is brimming with the bright flavor of fresh citrus and the nutty crunch of toasted walnuts. Mix things up a bit by substituting radicchio for some of the mixed greens or using attractive blood oranges instead of the navel variety.

DRESSING

- 1 tablespoon balsamic vinegar
- 2 teaspoons grated orange peel
- ¼ teaspoon salt
- ⅛ teaspoon freshly ground pepper
- 2 tablespoons extra-virgin olive oil

SALAD

- 3 cups torn Boston lettuce
- 3 cups mixed baby greens
- 2 navel oranges, cut into segments, segments halved
- 1 cup walnut halves, toasted*

1 In small bowl, whisk together vinegar, orange peel, salt and pepper. Whisk in oil.

2 In large bowl, combine lettuce and baby greens; toss with enough dressing to lightly coat. Divide among 6 salad plates; top with orange segments and walnuts.

TIP *To toast walnuts, place on baking sheet; bake at 375°F. for 4 to 6 minutes or until pale brown and fragrant. Cool.

8 (1¼-cup) servings

PER SERVING: 135 calories, 11.5 g total fat (1 g saturated fat), 3 g protein, 7 g carbohydrate, 0 mg cholesterol, 80 mg sodium, 2.5 g fiber

RECIPE BY JILL VAN CLEAVE

Tomatoes with Pesto and Asiago Cheese

Tomatoes with Pesto and Asiago Cheese

This tasty play on a caprese salad is a beautiful way to show off just-ripe tomatoes from your garden. If you want to be truly traditional, make the pesto with a mortar and pestle instead of a food processor. If using a food processor, pulse the mixture slowly so the oils from the nuts and basil are released gradually. In a pinch, substitute purchased pesto.

- ¼ cup pine nuts
- 2 garlic cloves
- 2 cups slightly packed fresh basil
- 4 oz. Asiago or Parmesan cheese, divided*
- ½ cup olive oil
- ¼ teaspoon salt
- ¼ teaspoon freshly ground pepper
- 4 tomatoes, sliced or cut into wedges

1 Place pine nuts in small skillet; cook over medium heat 2 minutes or until golden brown, stirring frequently. Cool.

2 Place pine nuts and garlic in food processor; pulse until finely chopped. Add basil; pulse until finely chopped.

3 Shred half of the cheese; add to food processor, pulsing to mix. Scrape bowl; with processor running, slowly add oil. Stir in salt and pepper. (Pesto can be made up to 2 days ahead. Cover and refrigerate.)

4 Arrange tomatoes on platter; top with pesto. With vegetable peeler, shave remaining cheese over pesto.

TIP *Asiago cheese is made from cow's milk and has a firm texture with a nutty flavor. It's similar to Parmesan cheese and can be grated or shredded.

8 (½-cup) servings

PER SERVING: 215 calories, 19.5 g total fat (4.5 g saturated fat), 7 g protein, 4.5 g carbohydrate, 10 mg cholesterol, 305 mg sodium, 1.5 g fiber

RECIPE BY JESSE COOL

Summer Bean and Pepper Salad

This very simple lemon- and cumin-spiked salad is an ideal vehicle for fresh summer produce. Serve it with grilled salmon or a flaky white fish, such as bass or flounder.

- 1 lb. green or yellow beans, halved diagonally
- 1 red bell pepper, thinly sliced
- 3 garlic cloves, minced
- 1 cup thinly sliced red onion
- ¼ cup extra-virgin olive oil
- 3 tablespoons red wine vinegar
- 2 tablespoons grated lemon peel
- 1 tablespoon sugar
- 1 tablespoon chopped fresh oregano
- 2 teaspoons ground cumin
- ½ teaspoon salt
- ¼ teaspoon freshly ground pepper

1 Cook beans in large pot of boiling water 2 to 3 minutes or until crisp-tender. Place in large bowl of ice water until cool. Drain well; place in large bowl.

2 Add all remaining ingredients; toss to combine. Let stand at room temperature at least 15 minutes. Toss again before serving.

10 (about ¾-cup) servings

PER SERVING: 75 calories, 5.5 g total fat (1 g saturated fat), 1 g protein, 7 g carbohydrate, 0 mg cholesterol, 125 mg sodium, 2 g fiber

RECIPE BY JESSE COOL

Tomato-Zucchini Gratin

When tomatoes and zucchini take over your garden, turn them into a hearty gratin. This one gets a nice, salty bite from Kalamata olives and crunch from an herb-laced bread crumb topping.

- 1 lb. tomatoes (about 3 medium), seeded, sliced (½ inch)
- 2 small zucchini, thinly sliced
- 1 teaspoon salt, divided
- ¾ cup fresh bread crumbs*
- ½ cup (2 oz.) lightly packed shredded Emmantaler or Gruyère cheese
- 1½ teaspoons herbes de Provence**
- 1½ teaspoons minced garlic
- ⅛ teaspoon freshly ground pepper
- 10 pitted Kalamata olives, quartered
- 5 teaspoons olive oil

1 Heat oven to 425°F. Spray 6-cup gratin or shallow ceramic or glass baking dish with nonstick cooking spray.

2 Arrange tomato and zucchini slices in single layer on paper towel-lined baking sheet. Sprinkle with ¾ teaspoon of the salt. Let stand 10 to 20 minutes. (Vegetables will begin to release moisture.) Pat gently with paper towels to dry.

3 Meanwhile, in medium bowl, toss together bread crumbs, cheese, herbes de Provence, garlic, remaining ¼ teaspoon salt and pepper until well-blended.

4 Layer tomato and zucchini slices alternately in gratin dish; top with olives. Sprinkle with bread crumb mixture; drizzle with oil.

5 Bake 18 to 20 minutes or until bread crumbs are browned and slightly crisp and gratin is heated through. Serve immediately.

TIPS *To make fresh bread crumbs, tear day-old whole-grain or white bread into pieces; place in food processor. Pulse 30 to 60 seconds or until coarse crumbs form. One bread slice yields about ¾ cup crumbs.

**Herbes de Provence can be found in the spice aisle of the grocery store. If you can't find it, substitute 1½ teaspoons dried basil, marjoram, rosemary, sage and/or thyme.

4 servings

PER SERVING: 170 calories, 12 g total fat (3.5 g saturated fat), 6.5 g protein, 11 g carbohydrate, 15 mg cholesterol, 785 mg sodium, 2 g fiber

RECIPE BY MARY EVANS

Grilled Southwest Potato Salad

Grilled Southwest Potato Salad

This picnic-perfect salad is imbued with nice smoky flavor, achieved by grilling the potatoes. Chile peppers give it a slight kick, but the heat is tempered by the cool sour cream dressing. The salad is best served the day it's made.

- 1 **lb. fingerling potatoes, unpeeled**
- 2 **tablespoons vegetable oil, divided**
- ½ **teaspoon ground cumin, divided**
- ½ **teaspoon salt, divided**
- ¼ **teaspoon freshly ground pepper, divided**
- 4 **green onions**
- 1 **large jalapeño chile**
- 2 **tablespoons white wine vinegar**
- ⅔ **cup halved grape tomatoes**
- ¼ **cup sour cream**
- 2 **teaspoons prepared mustard**
- 2 **tablespoons chopped cilantro**

1 Heat grill. Cut each potato crosswise into 2 to 4 pieces, depending on size. In shallow pan, stir together 1 tablespoon of the oil, ¼ teaspoon of the cumin, ¼ teaspoon of the salt and ⅛ teaspoon of the pepper. Add potatoes; toss to coat. Add green onions and chile; toss to coat.

2 Place potatoes and chile on gas grill over medium-high heat or on charcoal grill 4 to 6 inches from medium-high coals; cover grill. Grill 8 to 12 minutes or until evenly browned and tender, turning every 4 to 5 minutes. Add green onions; grill, uncovered, 4 minutes or until browned and tender, turning once. Place grilled vegetables in same shallow pan.

3 When cool enough to handle, halve potato pieces if desired. Peel chile; remove veins and seeds. Chop. Slice green onions. Place potatoes, chile and green onions in large bowl. Add vinegar and remaining 1 tablespoon oil, ¼ teaspoon cumin, ¼ teaspoon salt and ⅛ teaspoon pepper. Toss until well-mixed. Cool to room temperature.

4 Add tomatoes to potato mixture; toss. In small bowl, stir together sour cream, mustard and cilantro. Stir into potato mixture until thoroughly combined. Serve at room temperature.

4 (¾-cup) servings

PER SERVING: 195 calories, 10 g total fat (3 g saturated fat), 3 g protein, 25.5 g carbohydrate, 10 mg cholesterol, 615 mg sodium, 4 g fiber

RECIPE BY JILL VAN CLEAVE

Greens with Cherries and Walnuts

Contrasting flavors and textures make this salad irresistibly good. It partners well with a variety of grilled meats and seafood.

VINAIGRETTE

- ¼ cup finely chopped shallots
- ¼ cup white wine vinegar
- 1 tablespoon Dijon mustard
- ¾ teaspoon salt
- ½ teaspoon freshly ground pepper
- ½ cup light or regular olive oil
- 2 tablespoons walnut oil

SALAD

- 16 cups mixed salad greens
- 2 cups fresh cherries, pitted, halved
- 1 cup coarsely chopped toasted walnuts*
- 1 cup (4 oz.) crumbled Maytag blue or other blue-veined cheese

1 In small bowl, whisk together shallots, vinegar, mustard, salt and pepper. Whisk in olive oil and walnut oil until blended. Let stand 15 minutes. (Vinaigrette can be made up to 6 hours ahead.)

2 In large bowl, toss greens with enough vinaigrette to lightly coat. Add cherries and nuts; toss. Sprinkle with cheese.

TIP *To toast walnuts, place on baking sheet; bake at 375°F. for 4 to 6 minutes or until pale brown and fragrant. Cool.

8 (2-cup) servings

PER SERVING: 340 calories, 31 g total fat (6 g saturated fat), 7.5 g protein, 12.5 g carbohydrate, 10 mg cholesterol, 500 mg sodium, 4 g fiber

RECIPE BY MELANIE BARNARD

Souffléed Corn Pudding

This pudding is an excellent way to use corn cut fresh off the cob. The kernels stay slightly crisp during baking, providing an appealing contrast in an otherwise creamy soufflé. You can substitute a 1-pound bag of frozen corn kernels, which are cut from fresh cobs and frozen within hours of picking.

¼	cup unsalted butter
¼	cup all-purpose flour
2	cups half-and-half
4	eggs, separated
4	cups corn kernels (from 6 to 8 ears)
1	cup thinly sliced green onions
1½	tablespoons chopped fresh thyme
1	teaspoon salt
¾	teaspoon freshly ground pepper

1 Heat oven to 350°F. Generously butter shallow 2-quart (11×7- or 9×9-inch) glass or ceramic baking dish.

2 Melt butter in medium saucepan over medium heat. Whisk in flour; cook and stir 2 to 3 minutes or until mixture is smooth and begins to turn pale golden brown. Slowly whisk in half-and-half; cook, stirring constantly, 2 to 3 minutes or until mixture thickens and comes to a boil. Remove from heat.

3 Place egg yolks in large bowl. Whisk about one-third of the butter mixture into yolks; whisk yolk mixture back into remaining butter mixture. Cook and stir over medium-low heat 2 to 3 minutes or until sauce thickens. Pour into same large bowl; stir in corn, green onions, thyme, salt and pepper. Cool slightly, about 5 minutes.

4 Place egg whites in medium bowl; beat at medium-high speed until firm but not stiff peaks form. Stir about one-fourth of the whites into corn mixture. Gently fold in remaining whites until combined. Spoon into baking dish.

5 Bake 45 to 50 minutes or until pudding is puffed and golden brown with firm edges (center will be wobbly but will not run like liquid). Serve immediately (pudding will sink as it cools).

8 servings

PER SERVING: 245 calories, 16 g total fat (9 g saturated fat), 7.5 g protein, 21.5 g carbohydrate, 145 mg cholesterol, 355 mg sodium, 2.5 g fiber

RECIPE BY MELANIE BARNARD

Orange-Mint Fruit Salad

The beauty of this salad is its adaptability. Use any fresh fruit, such as cherries, apricots, nectarines, melons, grapes or berries. Cucumbers add a nice, crunchy contrast. You can prepare the salad in advance, but stir in the yogurt mixture just before serving.

- 1 medium cucumber, peeled, halved lengthwise
- 4 cups chopped mixed fresh fruit
- ¾ cup plain yogurt
- 2 tablespoons finely chopped fresh mint, divided
- 2 tablespoons sugar
- 2 tablespoons orange juice
- 2 teaspoon grated orange peel

Slide teaspoon down center of each cucumber half to remove seeds. Thinly slice cucumber; place in large bowl. Add fruit. In small bowl, stir together yogurt, 1 tablespoon of the mint, sugar, orange juice and orange peel. Pour over fruit mixture; toss lightly. Sprinkle with remaining 1 tablespoon mint.

8 (¾-cup) servings

PER SERVING: 80 calories, .5 g total fat (.5 g saturated fat), 2 g protein, 17.5 g carbohydrate, 0 mg cholesterol, 15 mg sodium, 1.5 g fiber

RECIPE BY JESSE COOL

Orange-Mint Fruit Salad

Cranberry-Wild Rice Pilaf

This recipe marries white and wild rice in a classic pilaf-style side dish. It's accented with sweet-tart dried cranberries and zesty lemon. Using basmati rice instead of white rice provides an even nuttier aroma and flavor.

½ cup wild rice
3 tablespoons butter
½ cup thinly sliced green onions
1 cup basmati or long-grain white rice
½ cup dried cranberries
2½ cups reduced-sodium chicken broth
¼ teaspoon salt
¼ teaspoon freshly ground pepper
¼ cup chopped fresh parsley
2 teaspoons grated lemon peel

1 In medium saucepan, bring 2 cups lightly salted water to a boil. Add wild rice; cook, covered, over medium-low heat 30 minutes. Drain; rinse under cold water.

2 Melt butter in large saucepan over medium heat. Add green onions; cook 2 to 3 minutes or until softened. Stir in basmati rice and dried cranberries; cook 3 minutes, stirring occasionally. Stir in wild rice. (Recipe can be made to this point up to 4 hours ahead. Cover and refrigerate.)

3 Add broth, salt and pepper; bring to a boil over high heat. Reduce heat to low; cover and simmer 15 minutes or until rice is tender. Remove from heat; let stand, covered, 5 minutes. Stir in parsley and lemon peel.

8 (½-cup) servings

PER SERVING: 200 calories, 5 g total fat (3 g saturated fat), 5 g protein, 35.5 g carbohydrate, 10 mg cholesterol, 280 mg sodium, 1.5 g fiber

RECIPE BY JILL VAN CLEAVE

Rice Duo

Blending rice varieties is an excellent way to give a dish a more complex personality. In Cranberry-Wild Rice Pilaf, the more delicately textured and lightly nutty-flavored basmati rice complements the chewy, bolder-tasting wild rice.

Basmati rice is a long-grain variety. The tastiest comes from India, where it's cultivated in the flood plains of the Himalayan foothills. Its unique flavor is derived from the soil in which it's grown and the aging of the rice. Look for it in well-stocked supermarkets and Asian stores.

Though its name suggests otherwise, wild rice isn't really a rice; it's the seed of an aquatic grass. And much of it isn't actually wild; most wild rice is cultivated. True wild rice tends to be more expensive than cultivated, but it also cooks more quickly, has a more nutty taste and is less chewy. You can find wild rice in most grocery stores.

Fall Salad with Apples, Almonds and Raisins

When dressing tossed salads like this one, be careful not to overdo it. Start by tossing the greens with a small amount of the vinaigrette and gradually add more, if needed. There should be no dressing pooling in the bottom of the bowl.

⅓ cup extra-virgin olive oil

3 tablespoons balsamic vinegar

2 teaspoons Dijon mustard

½ teaspoon salt

½ teaspoon freshly ground pepper

16 cups (10 oz.) loosely packed mixed salad greens

2 large apples, peeled, diced

¾ cup sliced almonds, toasted*

¾ cup golden raisins

1 In small bowl, whisk together oil, vinegar, mustard, salt and pepper.

2 Place all remaining ingredients in large bowl. Toss with enough vinaigrette to lightly coat.

TIP *To toast almonds, place on baking sheet; bake at 375°F. for 4 to 6 minutes or until light golden brown. Cool.

8 (2-cup) servings

PER SERVING: 200 calories, 13.5 g total fat (1.5 g saturated fat), 3 g protein, 20.5 g carbohydrate, 0 mg cholesterol, 195 mg sodium, 3 g fiber

RECIPE BY KAREN LEVIN

Walnut-Pear Salad with Cranberry Vinaigrette

A really fabulous dressing sets off this lovely harvest salad of pears and cranberries. Cranberry juice gives it a nice sweet-tart character, while walnut oil lends depth and wonderful nutty notes.

VINAIGRETTE

- ¼ cup thawed frozen cranberry juice concentrate
- 3 tablespoons red wine vinegar
- 2 teaspoons Dijon mustard
- ½ teaspoon salt
- ½ teaspoon freshly ground pepper
- 5 tablespoons walnut oil

SALAD

- 12 cups mixed salad greens
- ⅓ cup coarsely chopped walnuts, toasted*
- ¼ cup dried cranberries
- 1 red pear, unpeeled, sliced

1 In small bowl, whisk together all vinaigrette ingredients except oil. Slowly whisk in oil. Let stand at room temperature at least 15 minutes or refrigerate up to 24 hours; bring to room temperature before using.

2 Place all salad ingredients in large bowl. Toss with enough vinaigrette to lightly coat.

TIP *To toast walnuts, place on baking sheet; bake at 375°F. for 4 to 6 minutes or until pale brown and fragrant. Cool.

8 (1½-cup) servings

PER SERVING: 165 calories, 12 g total fat (1 g saturated fat), 2 g protein, 14.5 g carbohydrate, 0 mg cholesterol, 205 mg sodium, 2.5 g fiber

RECIPE BY MELANIE BARNARD

Gorgonzola-Balsamic Greens with Pepper-Glazed Pecans

Sweet, sour, spicy and salty flavors come together in this salad. The peppered pecans and Gorgonzola cheese lend upscale flair to a classic mixed-greens salad.

PECANS

¼ cup sugar

½ teaspoon freshly ground black pepper

¼ teaspoon salt

⅛ teaspoon cayenne pepper

2 tablespoons butter

1½ cups pecan halves

1 tablespoon balsamic vinegar

SALAD

2 tablespoons balsamic vinegar

1 teaspoon Dijon mustard

¼ teaspoon salt

6 tablespoons canola oil

12 cups torn mixed salad greens

8 oz. Gorgonzola cheese, crumbled

1 In medium bowl, stir together sugar, black pepper, ¼ teaspoon salt and cayenne pepper. Melt butter in large skillet over medium heat. Stir in pecans; cook and stir 2 minutes. Add 1 tablespoon balsamic vinegar; cook 1 minute or until vinegar has evaporated. Remove from heat. Add to spice mixture; toss to coat. Cool to room temperature.

2 In another small bowl, whisk together 2 tablespoons vinegar, mustard and ¼ teaspoon salt. Whisk in oil. Just before serving, in large bowl, toss greens with enough of the vinaigrette to lightly coat. Place on platter. Sprinkle with cheese; top with pecans.

8 (1¼-cup) servings

PER SERVING: 385 calories, 35 g total fat (9 g saturated fat), 9 g protein, 12 g carbohydrate, 30 mg cholesterol, 580 mg sodium, 3.5 g fiber

RECIPE BY MARY EVANS

Main Dishes

Peppered Beef Roast with
Cranberry-Red Wine Sauce

Peppered Beef Roast with Cranberry-Red Wine Sauce

A boneless beef sirloin tip roast is a tender and affordable cut. This elegant recipe acquires a savory crust during baking thanks to the rub and herb mixture spread over the outside. It's paired with a sweet-tart sauce that provides a nice counterpoint to the rich meat.

BEEF

- 1 (3-lb.) boneless beef sirloin tip roast
- 2 teaspoons Dijon mustard
- 2 teaspoons tomato paste
- 2 teaspoons minced garlic
- 1 teaspoon canola oil
- 1 tablespoon coarsely ground pepper
- 1 teaspoon dried thyme
- ¾ teaspoon dried rosemary
- ¾ teaspoon salt
- ¼ teaspoon ground coriander

SAUCE

- 1 tablespoon butter
- ¼ cup minced shallots
- 1 teaspoon sugar
- 1 cup red wine or cranberry juice
- 1 cup fresh or fozen cranberries
- ½ cup reduced-sodium beef broth

1 Heat oven to 350°F. Pat roast dry; place in heavy shallow roasting pan. In small bowl, stir together mustard, tomato paste, garlic and oil; rub over entire surface of roast. In another small bowl, stir together pepper, thyme, rosemary, salt and coriander; sprinkle over surface of roast. Bake 1 hour 25 minutes to 1 hour 35 minutes or until internal temperature reaches 140°F. for medium-rare or until of desired doneness.

2 Meanwhile, melt butter in medium saucepan over medium-low heat. Add shallots; cook 3 to 5 minutes or until shallots begin to brown. Sprinkle with sugar; cook 1 minute. Add wine, cranberries and broth. Increase heat to medium. Bring to a boil; gently boil 5 minutes. Strain into medium bowl, pressing on cranberries to extract pulp and scraping accumulated pulp on bottom of strainer into wine mixture, repeating pressing and scraping several times. (Sauce can be made up to 1 day ahead. Cover and refrigerate.)

3 Place roast on platter; cover loosely with foil. Let stand 10 to 20 minutes.

4 Meanwhile, add sauce to roasting pan. Bring to a boil over medium heat, scraping up any browned bits from bottom of pan; boil 1 to 2 minutes to combine flavors. Serve sauce with roast.

8 servings

PER SERVING: 235 calories, 7.5 g total fat (2.5 g saturated fat), 34.5 g protein, 4.5 g carbohydrate, 95 mg cholesterol, 355 mg sodium, 1 g fiber

RECIPE BY MARY EVANS

Meltingly Tender Pot Roast

This traditional-style pot roast is cooked smothered in onions, giving it a sweet, caramelized taste. Roasted carrots and Yukon Gold potatoes cook alongside the meat, making this a one-pot meal. For the best flavor, make sure to brown the brisket on all sides.

1	tablespoon olive oil
1	(2½- to 2¾-lb.) beef brisket (flat-cut or first-cut)
2	teaspoons dried thyme
½	teaspoon salt
½	teaspoon freshly ground pepper
1	tablespoon butter
4	large onions, halved, sliced (½ inch)
4	large garlic cloves, minced
¾	cup reduced-sodium beef broth
¾	cup red wine or additional beef broth
1	tablespoon Worcestershire sauce
4	medium carrots, cut into 2-inch pieces
4	medium Yukon Gold potatoes (1¾ lb.), unpeeled, quartered, or halved if small

1 Heat oven to 350°F. Heat heavy large pot over medium-high heat until hot. Add oil; heat until hot. Add brisket; cook 5 to 7 minutes or until browned, turning once. Place on plate; sprinkle both sides with thyme, salt and pepper.

2 Melt butter in pot over medium heat. Add onions; stir to coat with butter. Cover and cook 5 minutes or until wilted. Uncover; increase heat to medium-high. Cook 5 minutes or until onions start to brown, stirring occasionally. Add garlic; cook 30 seconds or until fragrant, stirring constantly. Stir in broth, wine and Worcestershire sauce.

3 Return brisket to pot; spoon onions over brisket. Cover; bake 1 hour. Turn brisket; spoon onions over brisket. Arrange carrots and potatoes around brisket. Cover; bake an additional 1 hour or until brisket and vegetables are tender when pierced with knife.

4 Place brisket on cutting board; cover loosely with foil. Let stand 10 to 15 minutes. Thinly slice brisket; serve with onions, potatoes and carrots. Spoon any accumulated pan juices over brisket.

6 servings

PER SERVING: 440 calories, 14.5 g total fat (5.5 g saturated fat), 37.5 g protein, 40.5 g carbohydrate, 70 mg cholesterol, 345 mg sodium, 6.5 g fiber

RECIPE BY JANICE COLE

Meltingly Tender Pot Roast

Short Ribs Jambalaya

While many ingredients in a Louisiana jambalaya are subject to variation, rice is essential. This one-pot dish features tender, boneless short ribs, which imbue the rice with a rich, meaty flavor. The finished jambalaya should be moist but not soupy. Have hot sauce available for those who prefer it spicy. Serve with Black Pepper Biscuits, page 31.

2	lb. boneless beef short ribs
4	teaspoons Creole or Cajun seasoning
½	teaspoon freshly ground pepper
2	tablespoons vegetable oil
1	onion, chopped
1	green bell pepper, chopped
½	cup chopped celery
2	large garlic cloves, minced
1	(28-oz.) can diced tomatoes, drained
4	cups reduced-sodium beef broth, divided
2	bay leaves
2	teaspoons chopped fresh thyme
2	cups long-grain white rice
8	green onions, thinly sliced
¼	cup chopped fresh parsley

1 Heat oven to 350°F. Cut ribs into 2-inch pieces. In small bowl, stir together Creole seasoning and pepper; sprinkle over ribs.

2 Heat oil in heavy large pot or Dutch oven over medium-high heat until hot. Add ribs in batches; cook 3 to 4 minutes or until browned, turning once. Place on plate.

3 Reduce heat to medium. Add onion, bell pepper, celery and garlic; cook 8 to 10 minutes or until softened, stirring occasionally. Return ribs and any accumulated juices to pot; add tomatoes, 2 cups of the broth, bay leaves and thyme. Increase heat to medium-high; bring to a boil.

4 Cover pot; place in oven. Bake 1½ hours or until meat is tender, stirring halfway through.

5 Remove from oven; return pot to stovetop. Uncover and stir in remaining 2 cups broth; bring to a boil over medium-high heat. Stir in rice, green onions and parsley; cover and return to oven. Bake 30 minutes or until rice is tender and liquid is absorbed. Let stand, covered, 5 minutes.

8 (1½-cup) servings

PER SERVING: 515 calories, 22 g total fat (7.5 g saturated fat), 29.5 g protein, 49.5 g carbohydrate, 90 mg cholesterol, 535 mg sodium, 2.5 g fiber

RECIPE BY JILL VAN CLEAVE

Short Ribs Jambalaya

Grilled Beef and Mushroom Kebabs

A final dab of anchovy-spiked butter adds a touch of pure decadence to this easy skewered meal. Simple preparation allows the meaty sirloin flavor to come through. Pair the skewers with garlic mashed potatoes, or serve them with grilled potato, zucchini or onion wedges.

MARINADE

- 3 tablespoons red wine or 2 tablespoons red wine vinegar
- 2 tablespoons Worcestershire sauce
- 1 tablespoon minced garlic
- 1 tablespoon freshly ground pepper
- 1 teaspoon dried rosemary
- 1 teaspoon balsamic vinegar
- 1 bay leaf, coarsely broken

BEEF

- 1½ lb. beef sirloin steak, cut into 1-inch pieces
- 24 crimini mushrooms*
- 2 tablespoons olive oil

BUTTER

- ½ cup butter, softened
- 1 tablespoon mashed anchovies or anchovy paste

1 In large bowl, stir together all marinade ingredients. Add steak and mushrooms; stir to coat with marinade. Cover and refrigerate at least 1 hour or overnight.

2 Meanwhile, in small bowl, stir together butter and anchovies.

3 Heat grill. Thread steak onto 4 (14-inch) metal skewers; thread mushrooms onto 2 (14-inch) metal skewers. Brush skewers with oil. Place on gas grill over medium heat or on charcoal grill 4 to 6 inches from medium coals; cover grill. Grill 8 to 10 minutes for medium-rare or until of desired doneness, turning to brown all sides. Serve skewers brushed with anchovy butter.

TIP *Crimini mushrooms look like brown button mushrooms and are often labeled as baby portobello mushrooms.

4 servings

PER SERVING: 495 calories, 36 g total fat (14.5 g saturated fat), 38.5 g protein, 5.5 g carbohydrate, 155 mg cholesterol, 375 mg sodium, 1.5 g fiber

RECIPE BY EBERHARD WERTHMANN

Flat Iron Steaks Grilled with Chile-Orange Marinade

Flat iron steaks, a fairly new variety, are one of the three most tender cuts of beef. They're also known as top blade steaks. Here, they acquire a fabulous smoky flavor from chopped chiles and chili powder. Serve them with a fruit salsa, if desired.

MARINADE

- 1 cup orange juice
- ¼ cup lemon juice
- ¼ cup olive or vegetable oil
- 1 jalapeño chile, veins and seeds removed, chopped
- 1 tablespoon chopped chipotle chile in adobo sauce*
- 2 tablespoons soy sauce
- 2 teaspoons grated orange peel
- 2 teaspoons grated lemon peel
- 2 teaspoons minced garlic
- 2 teaspoons chili powder
- 2 teaspoons kosher (coarse) salt
- 1 teaspoon freshly ground pepper

STEAK

- 4 (6-oz.) boneless beef flat iron, chuck-eye or top round steaks (1 inch thick)

1 In small bowl, stir together all marinade ingredients. Place steaks in 1-gallon resealable plastic bag; pour in marinade. Seal bag; turn to coat steaks. Refrigerate at least 12 hours or up to 24 hours, turning occasionally.

2 Heat grill. Remove steaks from marinade; discard marinade. Pat steaks dry. Place on gas grill over medium heat or on charcoal grill 4 to 6 inches from medium coals; cover grill. Grill 8 to 12 minutes for medium-rare or until of desired doneness, turning once. Place on platter; cover loosely with foil. Let stand 5 minutes.

TIP *Chipotle chiles are brown, dried, smoked jalapeño chiles with wrinkled skin. They come dried, pickled or canned in adobo sauce. Look for them in the Latin section of the supermarket.

4 servings

PER SERVING: 365 calories, 23 g total fat (8 g saturated fat), 35 g protein, 2.5 g carbohydrate, 105 mg cholesterol, 405 mg sodium, .5 g fiber

Flat Iron Steak

Named because its shape somewhat resembles an old-fashioned iron, this cut of beef is a relative newcomer. It comes from deep within the shoulder muscle, an area that until recently was simply used for ground or stew meat. Because of the way it's cut, the flat iron is a very tender piece of meat. Yet because of where it comes from, it's also relatively economical.

RECIPE BY BRUCE AIDELLS

Lamb Chops with
Green Olive Tapenade

Lamb Chops with Green Olive Tapenade

These chops are stuffed with a delectable green olive tapenade that's simple to prepare and more flavorful than the store-bought varieties. Use mild green olives, such as Picholine from Provence, or regular green olives that have been rinsed. Be sure not to overfill the chops with the tapenade; it's meant to be more of a flavoring than a stuffing. The tapenade also can be used as a spread for crackers or a dip for raw vegetables.

 4 lamb rib chops (1½ inches thick)
 ½ cup Green Olive Tapenade, divided (recipe follows)
 2 teaspoons olive oil, divided
 ½ teaspoon salt
 ½ teaspoon freshly ground pepper

1 To create a pocket, make small horizontal slit in chops, taking care not to cut past bone. Fill each pocket with 1 teaspoon of the tapenade. (Do not overfill.)

2 Brush chops with 1 teaspoon of the oil; sprinkle with salt and pepper. Heat remaining 1 teaspoon oil in heavy large nonstick skillet over medium-high heat until hot. Add chops, being careful not to overcrowd. Cook 4 to 6 minutes or until browned, turning once. Reduce heat to medium. Cover; cook 4 to 6 minutes or until lamb is pink in center for medium-rare or until of desired doneness, turning once.

3 Place chops on platter; top with remaining tapenade. Cover loosely with foil; let stand 5 minutes.

4 servings

PER SERVING: 385 calories, 27 g total fat (7 g saturated fat), 32.5 g protein,
2.5 g carbohydrate, 105 mg cholesterol, 770 mg sodium, 1.5 g fiber

Green Olive Tapenade

 3 tablespoons toasted slivered almonds*
 1 garlic clove
 ½ cup pitted green olives, such as Picholine**
 2 anchovy fillets
 1 tablespoon capers
 1 tablespoon extra-virgin olive oil

1 Place almonds in food processor; process until finely ground. Place in small bowl.

2 With food processor running, add garlic; process until chopped. Add olives, anchovies, capers and oil; pulse until very finely chopped (do not overprocess). Add ground almonds; pulse 2 or 3 times to blend. (Tapenade also can be made by hand.)

TIPS *To toast almonds, place on baking sheet; bake at 375°F. for 4 to 6 minutes or until light golden brown. Cool.

**Remove pits from olives by pressing olives with side of knife until olives split.

RECIPES BY BRUCE AIDELLS

Lamb Pot Roast Provençale

Fragrant herbs and low, slow cooking give the meat a rich, complex flavor. Slow-roasting, a common way to prepare lamb, in Provence, makes the meat melt-in-your-mouth tender.

- 1   tablespoon minced garlic
- 1   teaspoon dried rosemary
- ½   teaspoon dried thyme
- 1   (3½-lb.) boneless leg of lamb, tied
- ¼   teaspoon salt
- ⅛   teaspoon freshly ground pepper
- 1   tablespoon olive oil
- 1½ cups chopped onions
- 1   (14.5-oz.) can diced tomatoes, drained
- ½   cup white wine or reduced-sodium chicken broth
- 2   teaspoons herbes de Provence*

1 Heat oven to 300°F. Chop garlic, rosemary and thyme together until finely chopped. Untie leg of lamb; lay flat. Sprinkle inner surface with one-third of the garlic mixture; re-tie lamb. Sprinkle outside with salt and pepper.

2 Heat oil in Dutch oven or large pot over medium-high heat until hot. Add lamb; cook 15 minutes or until browned on all sides. Place lamb on plate. Add onions to Dutch oven; cook 3 to 4 minutes or until onions begin to soften. Add remaining two-thirds garlic mixture; cook 30 to 60 seconds or until fragrant. Stir in tomatoes and wine; bring to a simmer. Remove from heat.

3 Return lamb to Dutch oven; sprinkle with herbes de Provence. Cover and bake 2½ to 3 hours or until very tender and internal temperature reaches 180°F. Place lamb on platter; cover loosely with foil. Let stand 10 to 20 minutes before slicing. Serve lamb with pan juices.

TIP *Herbes de Provence is a combination of dried herbs that usually contains basil, thyme, fennel seeds, savory, lavender, marjoram, rosemary and sage. It can be found in the spice aisle of the grocery store. If you can't find it, substitute 2 teaspoons dried basil, marjoram, rosemary, sage and/or thyme.

10 servings

PER SERVING: 275 calories, 12.5 g total fat (4 g saturated fat), 34.5 g protein, 4 g carbohydrate, 110 mg cholesterol, 195 mg sodium, 1 g fiber

RECIPE BY MARY EVANS

Tequila-Lime Butterflied Leg of Lamb

If you're feeding a group of people who like their meat cooked to different degrees of doneness, butterflied leg of lamb is an ideal choice. Because of its varied thickness, the meat provides both thicker areas that are more rare and thinner areas that come out well-cooked.

½ cup chopped cilantro
½ cup lime juice
¼ cup tequila
¼ cup soy sauce
¼ cup olive oil
3 tablespoons minced garlic
3 tablespoons grated lime peel
2 tablespoons ground cumin
2 tablespoons chili powder
2 teaspoons salt
1 (4-lb.) butterflied leg of lamb

1 In medium bowl, stir together all ingredients except lamb. Place lamb in large resealable plastic bag; pour in marinade. Seal bag; turn to coat meat. Refrigerate up to 24 hours, turning occasionally.

2 When ready to grill, set up grill as follows. **For charcoal grills:** Heat 40 to 60 coals in center of grill to medium heat. Divide coals, placing half on each side of grill, leaving center open. Place drip pan between piles of coals. Place grates on grill 4 to 6 inches from coals. **For gas grills:** Light two outside sections, leaving middle section unlit. Or light one side and leave other side unlit. Place drip pan under grates on unlit side. Heat on high until hot. Reduce heat to medium.

3 Remove lamb from marinade; shake off excess. Discard marinade. (If desired, cut meat in half for easier handling.) Place lamb on grill over direct heat; cover grill. Grill 8 to 12 minutes or until browned on all sides, turning once.

4 Move lamb to unheated part of grill; cover grill. Grill 12 to 18 minutes or until internal temperature reaches 130°F. to 135°F. for medium-rare or until of desired doneness. Place on cutting board; cover loosely with foil. Let stand 10 minutes; thinly slice.

8 servings

PER SERVING: 250 calories, 12 g total fat (4 g saturated fat), 31.5 g protein, 1 g carbohydrate, 100 mg cholesterol, 345 mg sodium, .5 g fiber

RECIPE BY BRUCE AIDELLS

Chipotle-Stuffed Pork Tenderloin
with Orange-Onion

Chipotle-Stuffed Pork Tenderloin with Orange-Onion Salsa

Skillet-roasting pepitas (green pumpkin seeds) gives them lovely smokiness and takes only half the time of oven-roasting. The savory citrus salsa makes a perfect tangy partner for the pork.

4 tablespoons corn oil, divided	½ teaspoon plus ⅛ teaspoon ground cinnamon, divided
1 medium onion, finely chopped	
4 large plum tomatoes, seeded, chopped	½ teaspoon ground cloves
4 large garlic cloves, minced	¼ cup tomato paste
2 large canned chipotle chiles in adobo sauce, finely chopped*	¾ teaspoon salt, divided
	¾ teaspoon freshly ground pepper, divided
½ cup raisins, chopped	3 (¾-lb.) pork tenderloins
1 tablespoon balsamic vinegar	½ cup pepitas, toasted, chopped**
2 teaspoons sugar	Orange-Onion Salsa (pg. 80)

1 Heat 2 tablespoons of the oil in heavy large skillet over medium heat until hot. Add onion; cook 3 minutes or until softened. Add tomatoes, garlic, chiles, raisins, vinegar, sugar, ½ teaspoon of the cinnamon and cloves; cook 4 minutes or until tomatoes are just softened and juice evaporates. Stir in tomato paste; cook 2 minutes or until paste darkens slightly. Sprinkle with ¼ teaspoon of the salt and ¼ teaspoon of the pepper. Place in large bowl; cool completely. (Stuffing can be made up to 1 day ahead. Cover and refrigerate.)

2 To create tunnel through center of tenderloin for stuffing: With thin knife, make slit at one end of tenderloin; work knife in toward center (avoid cutting through sides of tenderloin). Repeat from other end, creating a slit all the way through center. Poke handle of long wooden spoon into slit to enlarge tunnel. Stir pepitas into tomato mixture; spoon into pastry bag or heavy resealable plastic bag. Fill pork with stuffing, working from both ends until pork is uniformly stuffed. Secure ends with toothpicks. Cover and refrigerate. (Pork can be made to this point up to 1 day ahead.)

3 Heat oven to 350°F. Sprinkle pork with remaining ½ teaspoon salt, ½ teaspoon pepper and ⅛ teaspoon cinnamon. Heat remaining 2 tablespoons oil in heavy large skillet over medium heat until hot. Add pork; cook 4 to 6 minutes or until browned, turning several times to brown on all sides. Place on large rimmed baking sheet. Bake 25 to 30 minutes or until internal temperature of pork reaches 145°F. (If tenderloins were stuffed and refrigerated, you may need to increase baking time 6 to 8 minutes.) Place on cutting board; cover loosely with foil. Let stand 5 minutes. Remove toothpicks; cut pork diagonally into ½-inch slices. Arrange slices over Orange-Onion Salsa.

TIPS *Chipotle chiles in adobo sauce can be found in the Hispanic foods section of most supermarkets. If desired, remove some or all of the seeds. Any remaining chipotle chiles can be covered and refrigerated about one week.

**To toast pepitas (green pumpkin seeds), place in dry skillet. Heat over medium heat 3 to 5 minutes, watching carefully, or until pepitas are lightly browned and begin to pop.

8 servings

PER SERVING: 425 calories, 18.5 g total fat (4 g saturated fat), 36 g protein, 32 g carbohydrate, 80 mg cholesterol, 450 mg sodium, 5 g fiber

RECIPE BY LANE CROWTHER

Orange-Onion Salsa

Serve with Chipotle-Stuffed Pork Tenderloin, page 79.

4 medium oranges
4 green onions, sliced
1 cup chopped white onion
1 cup chopped red onion
2 tablespoons honey
2 tablespoons finely grated orange peel
2 teaspoons chili powder
1 teaspoon ground cumin

Cut peel and pith from oranges; remove orange segments by cutting between the membranes over small bowl. Reserve ¼ cup of the orange juice that accumulates. In large bowl, stir together orange segments, reserved ¼ cup orange juice and all remaining salsa ingredients. Cover and refrigerate. (Salsa can be made up to 4 hours ahead.)

RECIPE BY LANE CROWTHER

Pork with Shallot Sauce

Whole-grain Dijon mustard with mustard seeds adds extra taste and texture to this warm shallot sauce, but it's the smooth-style Dijon mustard that keeps the vinegar and oil emulsified into the sauce.

PORK

- 4 thick-cut boneless pork loin chops
- ¼ teaspoon salt
- ⅛ teaspoon freshly ground pepper
- 1 tablespoon canola oil

SAUCE

- ¾ cup thinly sliced shallots
- 7 teaspoons cider vinegar, divided
- 2 tablespoons whole-grain Dijon mustard (preferably Maille brand)
- ½ teaspoon salt
- ⅛ teaspoon freshly ground pepper
- 3 tablespoons canola oil
- 2 tablespoons water
- 2 teaspoons Dijon mustard

1 Sprinkle pork with ¼ teaspoon salt and ⅛ teaspoon pepper. Heat large skillet over medium heat until hot. Add 1 tablespoon oil; heat until hot. Add pork; cook 10 to 12 minutes or until slightly pink in center, turning once. Place on platter; cover loosely with foil.

2 Add shallots to same skillet. (If pan seems dry, add an additional 1 tablespoon oil before adding shallots.) Cook over medium heat 2 to 3 minutes or until shallots begin to soften, stirring frequently. Reduce heat to low; stir in 5 teaspoons of the vinegar, whole-grain mustard, ½ teaspoon salt and ⅛ teaspoon pepper. Simmer 30 to 60 seconds or until vinegar evaporates.

3 Remove from heat; cool slightly 1 minute. Whisk in 3 tablespoons oil, water, 2 teaspoons mustard and remaining 2 teaspoons vinegar. Serve sauce over pork.

4 servings

PER SERVING: 330 calories, 23 g total fat (4 g saturated fat), 26 g protein, 4 g carbohydrate, 70 mg cholesterol, 740 mg sodium, 1 g fiber

RECIPE BY MARY EVANS

Fennel-Roasted Pork Rib Roast

Fennel seeds and fresh fennel lend anise flavor to a tender pork roast. At the end, the pan juices are cooked down and blended with a touch of butter for a luscious sauce. Reserve some of the bright green frilly fronds from the fresh fennel for a beautiful garnish.

PORK

- 1 (6-lb.) bone-in center-cut pork loin roast
- 4 teaspoons kosher (coarse) salt
- 2 teaspoons fennel seeds, ground*
- 1 teaspoon freshly ground pepper
- 1 medium fennel bulb, halved, thinly sliced (2 cups)**
- 2 tablespoons sugar
- 1 tablespoon olive oil
- 2 cups reduced-sodium chicken broth, hot
- 1 cup hot water

SAUCE

- ¼ cup water
- 2 tablespoons cornstarch
- ¼ cup unsalted butter, cut up

1 Heat oven to 425°F. Place roast on cutting board so that rib bones point up. Starting at tips of ribs, cut loin away from bones until bottom of loin is reached. Leave loin connected to flat bones that roast is standing on.

2 In small bowl, stir together salt, fennel seeds and pepper. Sprinkle inside of loin with half of the salt mixture; replace meat on bones. Place roast on rimmed baking sheet, bone side down; sprinkle with remaining salt mixture. Bake pork 30 minutes.

3 Meanwhile, in medium bowl, stir together sliced fennel, sugar and oil. Reduce oven temperature to 325°F. Spread sliced fennel mixture over top of roast; bake 30 minutes. Pour broth and 1 cup hot water into baking sheet. Bake an additional 40 to 50 minutes or until internal temperature reaches 145°F. Place roast on cutting board; cover loosely with foil. Let stand 10 to 15 minutes.

4 Meanwhile, pour pan juices into small saucepan; bring to a boil over medium-high heat. In small bowl, whisk together ¼ cup water and cornstarch; whisk into juices in saucepan. Reduce heat to medium-low; cook 1 minute or until slightly thickened. Whisk in butter; remove from heat. Cover.

5 Cut loin from bones. Thinly slice loin; serve with sauce.

TIPS *Grind fennel seeds using a spice grinder or mortar and pestle.

**Fennel is a vegetable with a bulbous base and long, feathery fronds that look similar to dill. It has a sweet, delicate, anise-like flavor. To use fennel, remove the fronds and save for garnish or discard. The bulb can be sliced or chopped.

8 servings

PER SERVING: 505 calories, 26.5 g total fat (10.5 g saturated fat), 55.5 g protein, 7.5 g carbohydrate, 170 mg cholesterol, 1040 mg sodium, 1 g fiber

RECIPE BY STEPHEN LARSON

Fennel-Roasted Pork Rib Roast

Rosemary Roasted Salmon

This recipe is one of the easiest and quickest ways to serve salmon; it cooks in just 10 minutes. During the summer, try one of the great wild salmon species, such as king, coho or sockeye.

1½ lb. salmon fillet (1 inch thick)
4 medium garlic cloves, minced
2 tablespoons olive oil
1 tablespoon country-style Dijon mustard
1 tablespoon finely chopped fresh rosemary
¼ teaspoon salt
¼ teaspoon freshly ground pepper

1 Heat oven to 475°F. Line small rimmed baking sheet with foil. Place salmon fillet, skin side down, on baking sheet.

2 In small bowl, stir together garlic, oil, mustard and rosemary. Sprinkle salmon with salt and pepper. Spoon rosemary mixture over salmon. Refrigerate 10 minutes.

3 Bake salmon 8 to 10 minutes or until it just begins to flake.

4 servings

PER SERVING: 310 calories, 16.5 g total fat (3.5 g saturated fat), 36.5 g protein, 1.5 g carbohydrate, 110 mg cholesterol, 340 mg sodium, 0 g fiber

RECIPE BY TIM LAUER

Rosemary Roasted Salmon

Citrus-Peppercorn-Spiked Tuna

Citrus-Peppercorn-Spiked Tuna

Fresh tuna, with its meaty texture and flavor, is like steak—it's great on its own, but it also welcomes highly seasoned rubs and marinades. In this recipe, a sweet-hot rub adds zesty flavor with little effort.

　1　tablespoon packed brown sugar
　1　teaspoon grated lemon peel
　1　teaspoon grated lime peel
　½　teaspoon paprika
　4　(6- to 8-oz.) tuna steaks (¾ inch thick)
　1　teaspoon freshly ground pepper
　¼　teaspoon salt
　1　tablespoon canola oil

1 In small bowl, stir together brown sugar, lemon peel, lime peel and paprika. Sprinkle tuna with pepper and salt; sprinkle citrus mixture over tuna, pressing lightly into flesh.

2 Heat heavy large skillet over medium-high heat until hot. Add oil; heat until hot. Add tuna; cook 4 to 5 minutes for medium-rare or until of desired doneness, turning once.

4 servings

PER SERVING: 290 calories, 12 g total fat (2.5 g saturated fat), 40 g protein, 4 g carbohydrate, 65 mg cholesterol, 215 mg sodium, .5 g fiber

RECIPE BY TIM LAUER

Crab and Shrimp Enchiladas

The closing of her favorite Mexican restaurant spurred life member Emily E. Lane to try to recreate a much-loved dish. It's full of shrimp and crab, and covered with a creamy cheese sauce.

¼	cup butter
¼	cup all-purpose flour
2	cups reduced-sodium chicken broth
2	cups (8 oz.) shredded Monterey Jack cheese
¾	cup half-and-half
¼	teaspoon salt
⅛	teaspoon freshly ground pepper
½	cup sour cream
2	(8-oz.) pkg. imitation crab
8	oz. frozen shelled, deveined cooked small shrimp (sometimes called salad shrimp), thawed
½	cup sliced green onions, divided
8	(8-inch) flour tortillas

1 Heat oven to 350°F. Spray 13×9-inch glass baking dish with nonstick cooking spray.

2 Melt butter in medium saucepan over medium heat. Whisk in flour until blended. Slowly whisk in broth. Bring to a gentle boil. Whisk in cheese, half-and-half, salt and pepper. Place sour cream in medium bowl; slowly whisk in 1 cup of the sauce. Whisk sour cream mixture into remaining sauce. Remove from heat.

3 In large bowl, stir together crab, shrimp, 1 cup of the sauce and ¼ cup of the green onions. Place ½ cup of the filling on each tortilla. Roll up; place in baking dish. Cover with remaining sauce. Bake 20 to 25 minutes or until hot. Let stand 5 minutes; sprinkle with remaining ¼ cup green onions.

8 servings

PER SERVING: 460 calories, 23.5 g total fat (12.5 g saturated fat), 27.5 g protein, 33 g carbohydrate, 130 mg cholesterol, 1180 mg sodium, 1.5 g fiber

RECIPE BY LIFE MEMBER EMILY E. LANE, ALAMEDA, CA

Lemon Chicken with Asparagus

Chicken tenderloins are a nice alternative to the more traditional chicken breasts. They're extremely tender and work well for quick cooking. When choosing asparagus, look for very thin spears, which will cook quickly. Fresh lemon juice adds a bright note to the pan sauce.

1	lb. chicken tenderloins, halved lengthwise
1½	tablespoons chopped fresh thyme, divided
2	teaspoons grated lemon peel, divided
¼	teaspoon salt
¼	teaspoon freshly ground pepper
2	tablespoons olive oil
8	oz. thin asparagus
2	tablespoons finely chopped shallots
½	cup reduced-sodium chicken broth
2	tablespoons lemon juice

1 Sprinkle chicken with ½ tablespoon of the thyme, 1 teaspoon of the lemon peel, salt and pepper.

2 Heat oil in large skillet over medium-high heat until hot. Add chicken; cook 3 to 5 minutes or until golden brown and no longer pink in center, turning once. Place on plate; cover loosely with foil.

3 Add asparagus and shallots to same skillet; cook over medium heat 1 minute or until shallots are softened and asparagus is almost crisp-tender, stirring occasionally. Increase heat to medium-high. Add broth. Bring to a boil; boil 2 to 3 minutes or until slightly reduced. Stir in remaining 1 tablespoon thyme, remaining 1 teaspoon lemon peel and lemon juice. Return chicken and any accumulated juices to skillet; cook 1 minute or until heated through.

4 (1½ -cup) servings

PER SERVING: 220 calories, 10.5 g total fat (2 g saturated fat), 27 g protein, 4 g carbohydrate, 70 mg cholesterol, 285 mg sodium, 1.5 g fiber

RECIPE BY MELANIE BARNARD

Chicken-Spinach Lasagna
with Artichokes

Chicken-Spinach Lasagna with Artichokes

This creamy white lasagna is layered with an appealing combination of chicken, artichokes, mushrooms and spinach. Two kinds of cheese and a luscious white sauce add rich, satisfying flavor. Prepare the lasagna in advance for low-stress entertaining.

LASAGNA

- 2 tablespoons butter
- 2 large garlic cloves, minced
- 1½ teaspoons dried oregano
- 1 lb. boneless skinless chicken thighs, cut into ¾-inch pieces
- 1 (14-oz.) can quartered artichoke hearts, drained
- 8 oz. crimini mushrooms, coarsely chopped*
- ¼ teaspoon salt
- ¼ teaspoon freshly ground pepper
- 12 no-boil lasagna noodles (from 9-oz. pkg.)
- 2 (9-oz.) pkg. frozen chopped spinach, thawed, squeezed dry
- 3 cups (12 oz.) shredded mozzarella cheese
- ¾ cup (3 oz.) freshly grated Parmesan cheese

SAUCE

- ½ cup butter
- ½ cup all-purpose flour
- 2 cups whipping cream
- 2 cups milk
- ¼ teaspoon salt
- ¼ teaspoon freshly ground pepper
- ⅛ teaspoon ground nutmeg

1 Melt 2 tablespoons butter in heavy large skillet over medium heat. Add garlic and oregano; cook 30 seconds or until fragrant. Add chicken, artichoke hearts, mushrooms, ¼ teaspoon salt and ¼ teaspoon pepper; cook 6 to 8 minutes or until chicken is no longer pink and mushrooms are soft. Cool.

2 Melt ½ cup butter in large saucepan over medium heat. Whisk in flour; cook 3 to 4 minutes or until bubbly all over with nutty smell, whisking constantly. Whisk in all remaining sauce ingredients. Bring to a boil, whisking frequently; boil 1 to 2 minutes or until sauce has thickened.

3 Heat oven to 350°F. Spray 13×9-inch pan with nonstick cooking spray. Spread 1 cup of the sauce in pan. Top with 4 lasagna noodles; spread with 1 cup of the sauce. Sprinkle with one-half of the chicken mixture; top with one-half of the spinach. Sprinkle with 1 cup of the mozzarella cheese and ¼ cup of the Parmesan cheese. Repeat layering, starting with lasagna noodles. Top with remaining 4 noodles, remaining 1 cup sauce, 1 cup mozzarella cheese and ¼ cup Parmesan cheese. (Lasagna can be made to this point up to 8 hours ahead. Cover and refrigerate. It may need an additional 10 to 15 minutes baking time.)

4 Bake, uncovered, 45 to 55 minutes or until golden brown and bubbling. (Cover with foil during last 5 to 10 minutes if top is browning too quickly.) Let stand 15 minutes before cutting.

TIP *Crimini mushrooms look like brown button mushrooms and are often labeled as baby portobello mushrooms.

12 servings

PER SERVING: 525 calories, 34 g total fat (20 g saturated fat), 26 g protein, 30 g carbohydrate, 115 mg cholesterol, 590 mg sodium, 4.5 g fiber

RECIPE BY LIZ CLARK

Chicken Breasts with
Garam Masala Vinaigrette

Chicken Breasts with Garam Masala Vinaigrette

This simple vinaigrette is punctuated by the warm, spicy flavor of cinnamon, one of the main ingredients in garam masala, an Indian seasoning blend. While versions can vary, the spice mixture also usually contains cumin, coriander, black pepper and cardamom; look for it in the spice aisle of your grocery store. Try the vinaigrette on grilled lamb, too.

VINAIGRETTE

- 2 tablespoons malt vinegar or cider vinegar
- 1 tablespoon water
- 1 tablespoon tomato paste
- 1 tablespoon garam masala
- 1 teaspoon sugar
- ½ teaspoon salt
- ¼ cup canola oil

CHICKEN

- 4 boneless skinless chicken breast halves
- ¼ teaspoon salt
- ⅛ teaspoon freshly ground pepper
- 1 tablespoon chopped fresh mint

1 In small bowl, whisk together all vinaigrette ingredients except oil. Slowly whisk in oil.

2 Heat broiler. Spray broiler pan with nonstick cooking spray. Sprinkle chicken with ¼ teaspoon salt and pepper. Place on broiler pan; broil 4 to 6 inches from heat 9 to 12 minutes or until no longer pink in center, turning once.

3 Spoon vinaigrette over chicken; sprinkle with mint.

4 servings

PER SERVING: 285 calories, 17.5 g total fat (2 g saturated fat), 27 g protein, 3.5 g carbohydrate, 75 mg cholesterol, 540 mg sodium, .5 g fiber

RECIPE BY MARY EVANS

Indian-Spiced Grilled Chicken

These extra-tender chicken breasts get their succulence from a spiced yogurt marinade. While they need to marinate for just 2 hours for delicious results, increasing the time will boost the flavor and tenderness. Serve with basmati or brown rice and steamed sugar snap peas.

- ½ **cup plain nonfat yogurt**
- 1 **tablespoon olive oil**
- 1 **large garlic clove, minced**
- 2 **teaspoons ground coriander**
- 2 **teaspoons ground cumin**
- 2 **teaspoons grated fresh ginger**
- ½ **teaspoon salt**
- ½ **teaspoon paprika**
- ⅛ **teaspoon cayenne pepper**
- 2 **boneless skinless chicken breast halves**
- 2 **tablespoons chopped cilantro**

1 In small bowl, stir together all ingredients except chicken and cilantro.

2 Place chicken in shallow dish; spread yogurt mixture over chicken, turning to coat all sides. Cover and refrigerate at least 2 hours or up to 24 hours.

3 Heat grill; oil grill grate. Place chicken on gas grill over medium heat or on charcoal grill 4 to 6 inches from medium coals; cover grill. Grill 8 to 10 minutes or until chicken is no longer pink in center, turning once. Serve sprinkled with cilantro.

2 servings

PER SERVING: 210 calories, 8.5 g total fat (2 g saturated fat), 28.5 g protein, 4 g carbohydrate, 75 mg cholesterol, 385 mg sodium, .5 g fiber

RECIPE BY KAREN LEVIN

Indian-Spiced Grilled Chicken

Country Ham and Potato Quiche

Country Ham and Potato Quiche

This combination of ham, cheese, eggs and potatoes—referred to as country-style, or fermière, *by the French—is an ideal way to use up leftover bits of ingredients.*

1	(9-inch) unbaked pie crust	¼	teaspoon freshly ground pepper
1	tablespoon butter	3	eggs
½	cup sliced green onions	¾	cup half-and-half
⅔	cup Southern-style diced frozen hash browns or diced cooked potatoes	⅔	cup diced ham (½ inch), divided
¼	teaspoon salt	¾	cup (3 oz.) shredded Emmantaler or Gruyère cheese

1 Heat oven to 425°F. Line 9-inch tart pan with removable bottom or quiche pan with crust; place on baking sheet. Line crust with foil; fill with pie weights, dried beans or rice.

2 Place baking sheet with tart pan in oven; bake 20 minutes or until set. Remove foil and weights. Return to oven; bake 4 to 8 minutes or until crust is golden brown. Reduce oven temperature to 375°F.

3 Meanwhile, melt butter in medium skillet over medium-high heat. Add green onions; cook 1 minute. Add potatoes, salt and pepper; cook 5 to 6 minutes or until browned, stirring occasionally.*

4 In medium bowl, whisk eggs until blended; whisk in half-and-half until well-combined.

5 Sprinkle potato mixture and ½ cup of the ham over bottom of crust; pour in egg mixture. Sprinkle with remaining ham and cheese.

6 Bake at 375°F. for 25 to 35 minutes or until set and knife inserted in center comes out clean. Cool on wire rack 10 minutes.

TIP *If using cooked potatoes, cook 3 to 4 minutes.

6 servings

PER SERVING: 435 calories, 29.5 g total fat (17 g saturated fat), 15 g protein, 26.5 g carbohydrate, 185 mg cholesterol, 535 mg sodium, 1.5 g fiber

Single Pie Crust

1¼	cups all-purpose flour
¼	teaspoon salt
½	cup unsalted butter, chilled, cut up
4	to 5 tablespoons ice water

1 In medium bowl, stir together flour and salt. With pastry blender or 2 knives, cut in butter until mixture resembles coarse crumbs with some pea-sized pieces. Add 3 tablespoons of the water; stir until dough begins to form, adding additional water 1 teaspoon at a time if necessary. Shape into flat round; cover and refrigerate 1 hour or freeze 15 minutes.

2 On lightly floured surface, roll dough into 12-inch round ⅛ inch thick.

RECIPES BY MARY EVANS

Spicy Two-Sausage Chili

The idea of pairing kale with beans and sausage comes from the classic Portuguese recipe called caldo verde. Both the sausage and the jalapeño chiles add heat. Garnish the chili with grated cheddar cheese, sour cream, finely chopped green onions and prepared tomato salsa.

1 lb. dried red kidney or pinto beans	4 small Anaheim chiles, roasted, chopped*
10 cups water	2 jalapeño chiles, veins and seeds removed, finely chopped
2 ribs celery, coarsely chopped	2 tablespoons paprika
2 bay leaves	2 teaspoons ground cumin
2 sprigs fresh thyme	2 teaspoons chopped fresh marjoram or oregano, or 1 teaspoon dried
1 lb. bulk Mexican-style (unsmoked) chorizo or hot Italian sausage	1 teaspoon salt
12 oz. smoked sausage links, such as linguica, Andouille or Polish sausage, sliced (¼ inch)	1 teaspoon freshly ground pepper
2 cups chopped onions	1 (28-oz.) can crushed tomatoes in puree
2 tablespoons minced garlic	2 cups kale, stems removed, chopped
1 red bell pepper, roasted, chopped*	

1 Place beans in large heavy pot or Dutch oven; add enough water to cover by 2 inches. Bring to a boil over medium-high heat; boil 1 minute. Cover and remove from heat; let stand 1 hour. Drain and rinse.

2 Return beans to pot; cover with 10 cups water. Add celery, bay leaves and thyme; bring to a boil over medium-high heat. Reduce heat to medium-low to low; cover and cook 1 to 1 ½ hours or until beans are tender. Drain, reserving 4 cups of the liquid. Discard remaining liquid, celery, bay leaves and thyme.

3 Heat clean large pot or Dutch oven over medium-high heat. Add chorizo and smoked sausage; cook 5 minutes or until browned, stirring frequently. Add onions and garlic; cover and cook 5 minutes or until onions are soft, stirring frequently. Add bell pepper, Anaheim chiles, jalapeño chiles, paprika, cumin, marjoram, salt and pepper. Stir 1 minute or until vegetables are coated with spices.

4 Add tomatoes, beans and 4 cups reserved bean cooking liquid; bring to a boil. Reduce heat to medium-low; cook 15 minutes. Stir in kale; cook 15 minutes or until slightly thickened.

TIP *To roast bell peppers and chiles, place over high heat on gas or electric burner. Cook, turning with tongs occasionally, until skins are completely blackened. Place peppers and chiles in heavy plastic bag; close bag and let stand 15 minutes or until cool enough to handle. Peel blackened skins under running water. Slit peppers and chiles; remove veins and seeds.

10 (1½-cup) servings

PER SERVING: 490 calories, 25 g total fat (9 g saturated fat), 28 g protein, 41 g carbohydrate, 60 mg cholesterol, 1360 mg sodium, 11 g fiber

RECIPE BY BRUCE AIDELLS

Spicy Two-Sausage Chili

Beef and Mushroom Soup

Two types of mushrooms, plus the liquid used to soak the dried porcini mushrooms, imbue this beefy soup with deep mushroom flavor. The hearty stock gets extra richness from a touch of brandy.

1	oz. dried porcini or shiitake mushroom caps
2½	cups hot water
2	tablespoons vegetable oil, divided
1¼	lb. beef sirloin steak, cut into ¾-inch pieces
2	leeks, white and pale green parts only, chopped
2	medium russet potatoes, peeled, cut into ½-inch pieces
1	rib celery, chopped
10	oz. button mushrooms, sliced (4 cups)
3	garlic cloves, minced
3	tablespoons brandy, if desired
1	tablespoon tomato paste
½	teaspoon dried thyme
4	cups reduced-sodium beef broth
½	teaspoon kosher (coarse) salt

1 Place dried mushrooms and hot water in medium bowl; let stand 30 minutes or until soft. Remove mushrooms with slotted spoon; chop. Strain soaking liquid; reserve.

2 Meanwhile, heat 1 tablespoon of the oil in heavy large pot over medium-high heat until hot. Add beef; cook 5 to 7 minutes or until browned on all sides. Place beef on plate.

3 Heat remaining 1 tablespoon oil in same pot over medium-high heat until hot. Add leeks, potatoes, celery, button mushrooms and garlic; cook 10 minutes or until mushrooms release juices and vegetables soften, stirring frequently. Add brandy; boil 1 minute. Stir in tomato paste and thyme. Stir in broth, 2 cups of the reserved mushroom soaking liquid and salt; bring to a boil. Reduce heat to medium-low; simmer 25 minutes.

4 Stir in dried mushrooms, beef and any accumulated juices; simmer 2 minutes or until heated through.

6 (about 1¾-cup) servings

PER SERVING: 285 calories, 9 g total fat (2 g saturated fat), 28.5 g protein, 23.5 g carbohydrate, 55 mg cholesterol, 315 mg sodium, 3 g fiber

RECIPE BY LISA ZWIRN

Two-Bean Soup with Lentils

"When I was growing up, my mother made lentil soup and macaroni every week," says life member Russell C. Calaty. "It was a simple dinner the whole family enjoyed." He expanded on this favorite soup by adding beans to make it more nutritious. To enhance it even further, add cooked macaroni.

1 tablespoon olive oil
3 medium carrots, diced
2 ribs celery with leaves, diced
½ cup chopped onion
3 garlic cloves, minced
7 cups reduced-sodium chicken broth
1 (15-oz.) can garbanzo beans, drained, rinsed
1 (15-oz.) can kidney beans, drained, rinsed
1 (14.5-oz.) can whole tomatoes
1 cup uncooked lentils
1 tablespoon dried basil
1 teaspoon salt
½ teaspoon freshly ground pepper
1 (10-oz.) pkg. frozen spinach

Heat oil in large pot or Dutch oven over medium-high heat until hot. Add carrots, celery, onion and garlic; cook 5 minutes. Stir in broth, garbanzo beans, kidney beans, tomatoes, lentils, basil, salt and pepper. Bring to a boil; add spinach. Boil 10 minutes or until spinach has thawed. Reduce heat to low; simmer 35 minutes, breaking up tomatoes as they cook.

6 (about 2-cup) servings

PER SERVING: 330 calories, 4.5 g total fat (.5 g saturated fat), 23 g protein, 53 g carbohydrate, 0 mg cholesterol, 1385 mg sodium, 15 g fiber

RECIPE BY LIFE MEMBER RUSSELL C. CALATY, POLK CITY, FL

Hearty Chicken Noodle Soup

This satisfying version of chicken noodle soup puts the emphasis on chicken, with a generous amount in each spoonful. Fresh tarragon, with its pleasant anise flavor, adds a taste twist. To avoid having the noodles absorb all the broth, they're placed in the bottom of the serving bowls and then covered with the soup instead of being added directly to the pot.

1	(3- to 4-lb.) chicken, cut up
16	cups cold water
1	tablespoon kosher (coarse) salt
1	teaspoon freshly ground pepper
1	medium onion, coarsely chopped
½	teaspoon dried thyme
2	leeks, white and light green parts only, chopped
1	large carrot, coarsely chopped
1	parsnip, coarsely chopped
1	large rib celery, coarsely chopped
2	tablespoons finely chopped fresh tarragon
2	tablespoons finely chopped fresh parsley
2	cups wide egg noodles
½	cup (2 oz.) freshly grated Parmesan cheese

1 Place chicken, water, salt and pepper in large pot; bring to a boil over high heat. Skim surface; stir in onion and thyme. Reduce heat to medium to medium-low; partially cover and cook 1½ to 2 hours or until meat is falling off bones.

2 Remove chicken with slotted spoon. When cool enough to handle, remove chicken from bones. Meanwhile, skim off any grease from top of stock. Add leeks, carrot, parsnip and celery; cook 10 to 15 minutes or until vegetables are tender. Stir in chicken, tarragon and parsley; simmer 2 minutes or until heated through.

3 Meanwhile, cook noodles in large pot of boiling salted water according to package directions; drain.

4 To serve, place noodles in bottom of soup bowls; top with hot soup. Sprinkle with cheese.

8 (about 2-cup) servings

PER SERVING: 210 calories, 7 g total fat (2.5 g saturated fat), 21.5 g protein, 15.5 g carbohydrate, 65 mg cholesterol, 830 mg sodium, 2 g fiber

RECIPE BY LISA ZWIRN

Hearty Chicken Noodle Soup

French Onion Soup for Two

French Onion Soup for Two

This soup's wonderful richness is achieved by cooking the onions over low heat for an extended period of time. Avoid the temptation to speed up the process by increasing the heat; you'll lose some of the depth of flavor and could burn the onions. The recipe easily can be doubled.

- 2 tablespoons butter
- 1 very large sweet yellow onion, thinly sliced (4 cups)
- 1 tablespoon minced garlic
- ½ cup dry white wine
- 1 tablespoon all-purpose flour
- 2 (14-oz.) cans reduced-sodium beef broth
- ½ teaspoon dried thyme
- ¼ teaspoon freshly ground pepper
- 4 slices French bread (½ inch thick)*
- 1 cup (4 oz.) shredded Gruyère or Swiss cheese

1 Melt butter in large skillet over medium to medium-low heat. Add onion; cook 40 to 50 minutes or until dark golden brown, stirring frequently. (Reduce heat to low if cooking too fast.) Add garlic; cook 30 to 60 seconds or until fragrant. Add wine. Increase heat to medium-high; cook 1 minute or until nearly evaporated.

2 Stir in flour; cook and stir 1 minute. Stir in broth, thyme and pepper; bring to a boil. Reduce heat to medium-low; simmer 20 to 30 minutes to blend flavors.

3 Heat oven to 475°F. Place 2 ovenproof bowls on baking sheet; ladle soup into bowls. Top each serving with 2 bread slices and ½ cup cheese. Bake 10 to 15 minutes or until cheese is browned and bubbly.

TIP *Set out bread to dry while soup is cooking.

2 (2-cup) servings

PER SERVING: 630 calories, 34 g total fat (19 g saturated fat), 31 g protein, 53 g carbohydrate, 95 mg cholesterol, 790 mg sodium, 6 g fiber

RECIPE BY ELLEN BOEKE

Desserts

Raspberry-Nectarine Pie

Raspberry-Nectarine Pie

There's no need to peel the nectarines, and you don't have to worry about making a picture-perfect lattice topping; the colorful filling softens the edges of even the most rough-hewn crisscross as it bubbles up. Tapioca is the thickener of choice because it cooks up clear and glossy, allowing the bright colors of the fruit to shine. Serve the pie with whipped cream.

CRUST

- 1 **recipe Old-Fashioned Flaky Pie Crust (pg. 112)**
- 1 **tablespoon milk**
- 2 **teaspoons sugar**

FILLING

- 1 **cup sugar**
- 3 **tablespoons quick-cooking tapioca**
- ½ **teaspoon ground nutmeg**
- ¼ **teaspoon ground cardamom**
- 5 **large firm but ripe nectarines, sliced (½ inch) (7 cups)**
- 1 **pint (2 cups) raspberries**
- 1 **tablespoon lemon juice**

1 Place oven rack on lowest level; place baking sheet on rack. Heat oven to 425°F. Divide pie dough in half; refrigerate 1 piece. On lightly floured surface, roll remaining piece into 12-inch round. (Edge can be rough and you can pinch together any tears.) Roll dough over rolling pin; unroll into 9-inch pie pan. Let dough hang over edge of pan.

2 In large bowl, stir together 1 cup sugar, tapioca, nutmeg and cardamom. Add nectarines, raspberries and lemon juice; stir gently to combine. Spoon filling into pie crust. Refrigerate while rolling out lattice.

3 On lightly floured surface, roll remaining dough into 12-inch round. Cut into 5 (1¼-inch) strips. Place 3 strips lengthwise over pie; trim edges to inside of pie pan. Place remaining 2 strips crosswise over pie; trim edges. Fold edge of bottom crust over edges of strips. Brush dough with milk; sprinkle with 2 teaspoons sugar.

4 Place pie on baking sheet; bake at 425°F. for 30 minutes. Reduce oven temperature to 400°F. (If crust is brown, cover with foil, leaving center open for steam.) Bake at 400°F. for 15 minutes. Reduce oven temperature to 375°F.; bake an additional 15 to 25 minutes or until juices are bubbly and crust is rich golden brown. Cool on wire rack.

8 servings

PER SERVING: 530 calories, 22.5 g total fat (10 g saturated fat), 6 g protein, 80.5 g carbohydrate, 30 mg cholesterol, 300 mg sodium, 6.5 g fiber

RECIPE BY MELANIE BARNARD

Lemon-Blueberry Cobbler Pie

Lemon-Blueberry Cobbler Pie

Cobblers often are topped with biscuit dough, but this recipe relies on the old-fashioned version where pieces of pastry are placed over the fruit. They form a cobbled effect as the berries bubble over during baking. Serve it with vanilla ice cream.

CRUST
- 1   recipe Old-Fashioned Flaky Pie Crust (pg. 112)
- 1   tablespoon milk
- 2   teaspoons sugar

FILLING
- ⅔   cup sugar
- 3   tablespoons all-purpose flour
- 1½   teaspoons grated lemon peel
- ¾   teaspoon ground cinnamon
- 2   pints (4 cups) blueberries
- 2   teaspoons lemon juice

1 Place oven rack on lowest level; place baking sheet on rack. Heat oven to 425°F. On lightly floured surface, roll pie dough into 16-inch round. (Edge can be rough and you can pinch together any tears.) Cut into 14-inch round. Roll dough over rolling pin; unroll into 9½-inch deep-dish pie pan. Let dough hang over edge of pan. Cut dough scraps into rough 2-inch pieces.

2 In large bowl, stir together ⅔ cup sugar, flour, lemon peel and cinnamon. Add blueberries and lemon juice; stir to combine.

3 Spoon filling into crust. Fold edge of bottom crust over filling; top with dough scraps (they may touch but not overlap). Brush dough with milk; sprinkle with 2 teaspoons sugar.

4 Place pie on baking sheet; bake at 425°F. for 30 minutes. Reduce oven temperature to 400°F. (If crust is brown, cover with foil, leaving center open for steam.) Bake at 400°F. for 15 minutes. Reduce oven temperature to 375°F.; bake an additional 15 to 25 minutes or until juices are bubbly and crust is rich golden brown. Cool on wire rack.

8 servings

PER SERVING: 450 calories, 22 g total fat (10 g saturated fat), 5 g protein, 60 g carbohydrate, 30 mg cholesterol, 305 mg sodium, 3.5 g fiber

RECIPE BY MELANIE BARNARD

Old-Fashioned Flaky Pie Crust

Two different fats contribute to this crust's flaky texture. Vegetable shortening melts slower than butter, creating extra flakiness, and butter adds richness and superb flavor. But the secret ingredient is cider vinegar, which breaks down the gluten in the flour for a tender, more delicate crust.

2½ cups all-purpose flour	6 tablespoons shortening, chilled, cut up
1 teaspoon salt	5 to 7 tablespoons ice water
8 tablespoons unsalted butter, chilled, cut up	1½ teaspoons cider vinegar

In large bowl, stir together flour and salt. With pastry blender or 2 knives, cut in butter and shortening until mixture resembles coarse crumbs with some pea-sized pieces. Slowly add 5 tablespoons of the water and vinegar, stirring until dough just begins to come together. (If dough is too dry, sprinkle with additional water.) (Dough also can be made in food processor.) Form into flat round. Cover and refrigerate at least 1 hour or up to 2 days.

1 (9-inch) double-crust pie crust

PER 1/8 OF RECIPE: 330 calories, 21.5 g total fat (10 g saturated fat), 4 g protein, 30 g carbohydrate, 30 mg cholesterol, 295 mg sodium, 1 g fiber

---

Pie-making Tips

These fruit pies can be assembled quickly and easily. Here are some strategies to make the process go smoothly:

- Be sure the butter and shortening for the crust are well-chilled. If the dough is too soft, it will be more like cookie dough and not as flaky.

- Don't skimp on the flour when rolling out the pastry. The dough has plenty of shortening and will be flaky, even if you heavily flour the board and your hands.

- Be firm when you use the rolling pin. First pound the dough with the rolling pin to flatten it, then roll from the center of the dough outward to the desired size. Lift up the pastry and flour the board during rolling to keep the pastry from sticking.

- Don't worry about ragged edges or tears or holes in the dough. They can be patched with scraps.

- For a crisp, richly browned top crust, brush it with a little milk and sprinkle with sugar just before baking.

Generously flour the rolling surface and pin to make it easier to handle the dough.

If a hole develops in the crust, dampen the hole's outer edge with water and lightly press a scrap piece over it.

For a nicely browned top crust, brush it with milk and sprinkle with sugar before baking.

RECIPE BY MELANIE BARNARD

Maple-Nut Pie

This fabulously nutty pie calls for three types of nuts, toasted to intensify their flavors. The caramel-like filling is sweetened with maple syrup, a terrific flavor partner for the nuts. If you're feeling decadent, serve slices with a scoop of vanilla ice cream or softly whipped cream.

CRUST

1½	cups all-purpose flour
1	tablespoon sugar
⅛	teaspoon salt
¾	cup unsalted butter, chilled, cut up
2	tablespoons ice water

FILLING

1	cup walnut halves, toasted*
1	cup pecan halves, toasted*
1	cup whole hazelnuts, toasted*

6	egg yolks
½	cup sugar
½	cup packed dark brown sugar
½	cup pure maple syrup
⅓	cup unsalted butter
⅓	cup whipping cream
½	teaspoon salt
1	tablespoon brandy, if desired
1	teaspoon vanilla extract

1 In medium bowl, whisk together flour, 1 tablespoon sugar and ⅛ teaspoon salt. With pastry blender or 2 knives, cut in ¾ cup butter until mixture resembles coarse crumbs with some pea-sized pieces. Add water; stir until dough begins to form. Shape into flat round. Cover and refrigerate 30 minutes.

2 On lightly floured surface, roll dough into 12-inch round. Carefully place in 9-inch pie pan. Trim dough, leaving ½-inch overhang. Fold edge under, even with rim of pie pan; crimp. Poke bottom and sides of crust with fork every ½ inch. Freeze 20 minutes or until ready to bake.

3 Meanwhile, heat oven to 350°F. Line crust with foil; fill with pie weights or dried beans. Bake 20 minutes. Remove foil and weights; bake an additional 15 to 20 minutes or until crust is light golden brown. (If pastry begins to puff, poke lightly with fork.) Cool on wire rack about 30 minutes.

4 Place walnuts, pecans and hazelnuts in crust. Place egg yolks, ½ cup sugar, brown sugar, maple syrup, ⅓ cup butter, cream and ½ teaspoon salt in medium saucepan. Cook over medium-low heat, stirring constantly, until slightly thickened and mixture coats back of spoon or until temperature reaches 160°F. Do not boil. Immediately pour through fine strainer. Stir in brandy and vanilla. Pour over nuts (crust will be full).

5 Bake 40 to 50 minutes or until golden brown and slightly puffed. Cool on wire rack until warm. Serve slightly warm.

TIP *To toast nuts, place on baking sheet; bake at 350°F. for 6 to 8 minutes (walnuts and pecans) or 7 to 9 minutes (hazelnuts). Cool.

8 servings

PER SERVING: 810 calories, 59 g total fat (21 g saturated fat), 10.5 g protein, 66 g carbohydrate, 230 mg cholesterol, 205 mg sodium, 4.5 g fiber

RECIPE BY LISA SALTZMAN

Rhubarb-Strawberry Streusel Tart

Rhubarb and strawberries are a perfect spring marriage. In this tart, they're topped with a brown sugar streusel that uses chopped pecans to provide an appealing crunch.

Dough for 1 (9- to 10-inch) pie crust
3 cups sliced rhubarb (¾ inch)
3 cups strawberries, halved if large
1½ cups sugar
¼ cup cornstarch
¼ cup all-purpose flour
¼ cup packed brown sugar
2 tablespoons butter, softened
¼ cup finely chopped pecans

1 Heat oven to 375°F. Line 10-inch tart pan with removable bottom or ceramic pan with dough; trim edges. Place on rimmed baking sheet.

2 In large bowl, stir together rhubarb, strawberries, sugar and cornstarch; place in crust.

3 In medium bowl, stir together flour and brown sugar. With pastry blender or 2 knives, cut in butter until mixture resembles coarse crumbs with some pea-sized pieces. Stir in pecans. Sprinkle over tart. Place tart with baking sheet in oven; bake 55 to 65 minutes or until edges and center are bubbly and streusel is golden brown.

8 servings

PER SERVING: 355 calories, 11 g total fat (3.5 g saturated fat), 2.5 g protein, 64.5 g carbohydrate, 10 mg cholesterol, 125 mg sodium, 2.5 g fiber

RECIPE BY MEMBER KATHY SAWYER, GRAND RAPIDS, MI

Rhubarb-Strawberry Streusel Tart

Chocolate Angel Food Cake with Triple-Chocolate Glaze

CAKE

- ¼ cup Dutch-processed cocoa
- ¼ cup hot water
- ¾ cup all-purpose flour
- ½ cup powdered sugar
- ¼ teaspoon salt
- 1½ cups egg whites (10 to 12 large), cooled to room temperature
- 1½ teaspoons cream of tartar
- 1 teaspoon vanilla extract
- 1¼ cups superfine sugar

SEMISWEET CHOCOLATE GLAZE

- 4 oz. semisweet chocolate, chopped
- 4 tablespoons unsalted butter, softened, cut up
- 1 tablespoon light corn syrup

MILK CHOCOLATE GLAZE

- 2 oz. milk chocolate, chopped
- 2 tablespoons unsalted butter, softened, cut up
- 1½ teaspoons corn syrup

WHITE CHOCOLATE GLAZE

- 2 oz. white chocolate, chopped
- 2 tablespoons unsalted butter, softened, cut up
- 2 teaspoons whipping cream
- 1½ teaspoons corn syrup

1 Heat oven to 350°F. In small bowl, stir together cocoa and hot water until cocoa is dissolved.

2 Place flour, powdered sugar and salt in medium bowl. Sift 3 times to evenly distribute ingredients. Place egg whites in large bowl; beat at medium-low speed until loose and foamy. Add cream of tartar and vanilla; beat at medium-high speed until soft peaks just begin to form. With mixer running, slowly add superfine sugar in steady stream, beating just until egg whites are glossy and hold peaks that slightly bend at the tip. (Do not overbeat; peaks should not be dry and stiff.) Place about 1 cup of the egg white mixture in small bowl. Add cocoa mixture; stir until thoroughly combined.

3 Place chocolate mixture over remaining egg white mixture. Immediately sift one-third of the flour mixture over chocolate mixture; gently fold to incorporate. Repeat with remaining flour mixture, making sure no lumps of flour remain but being careful egg whites do not deflate. Gently spoon mixture into ungreased 10-inch tube pan with removable bottom. Run long narrow spatula through cake to eliminate any large air bubbles; gently smooth top. Bake 35 to 40 minutes or until cake springs back when gently touched and skewer inserted in center comes out clean. (Top may crack as it bakes.) Invert cake onto neck of bottle or funnel, or let stand upside-down on feet attached to tube pan. Cool completely in pan 2 to 3 hours.

4 To remove cake from pan, slide thin narrow knife or spatula around edges of pan and tube. Lift tube out of pan; invert cake onto serving platter.

5 Place all semisweet chocolate glaze ingredients in small saucepan. Heat over low heat, stirring constantly, until chocolate is melted and smooth. Remove from heat; let stand until slightly thickened. Drizzle over cake. Place all milk chocolate glaze ingredients in small saucepan. Heat over low heat, stirring constantly, until chocolate is melted and smooth. Remove from heat; let stand until slightly thickened. Drizzle over cake.Place all white chocolate glaze ingredients in small saucepan. Heat over low heat, stirring constantly, until chocolate is partially melted. Remove from heat; continue stirring until chocolate is melted and smooth. Let stand until slightly thickened; drizzle over cake.

12 servings

PER SERVING: 325 calories, 14 g total fat (8.5 g saturated fat), 5.5 g protein, 47.5 g carbohydrate, 25 mg cholesterol, 115 mg sodium, 1.5 g fiber

RECIPE BY JANICE COLE

Chocolate Angel Food Cake
with Triple-Chocolate Glaze

Maple-Pecan Layer Cake

Maple-Pecan Layer Cake

This two-layer cake is loaded with pecans and topped with a buttery, creamy frosting. While the nuts can be ground in a food processor, using a nut grater will produce a darker, nuttier taste because the more finely ground nuts are better dispersed throughout the cake. If possible, use grade B maple syrup; it's darker in color and has a stronger maple flavor.

CAKE

- ⅔ cup unsalted butter, softened
- 1⅓ cups sugar
- 4 eggs
- 1½ teaspoons vanilla extract
- 1 cup all-purpose flour
- ½ teaspoon salt
- ½ teaspoon baking soda
- ¼ teaspoon baking powder
- 1 cup finely grated or ground toasted pecans*
- ⅔ cup sour cream

FROSTING

- 3 cups powdered sugar, sifted
- ½ cup unsalted butter, softened
- ½ cup maple syrup
- ¼ cup finely chopped toasted pecans**

1 Heat oven to 350°F. Grease 2 (9×2-inch) round pans. Line bottoms with parchment paper; grease paper.

2 In large bowl, beat ⅔ cup butter and sugar at medium speed 4 to 5 minutes or until light and creamy. In small bowl, whisk together eggs and vanilla; beat into butter mixture in two parts.

3 In medium bowl, whisk together flour, salt, baking soda and baking powder. Whisk in 1 cup pecans. At low speed, beat into butter mixture in 3 parts alternately with sour cream, beginning and ending with flour mixture. Divide batter evenly between pans.

4 Bake 30 minutes or until golden brown and toothpick inserted in center comes out clean. Cool on wire rack 10 minutes. Invert cakes onto wire rack; remove parchment. Cool completely.

5 Meanwhile, in medium bowl, beat powdered sugar and ½ cup butter at medium-low speed until blended. Slowly beat in maple syrup until smooth and creamy.

6 Spread half of the frosting over one cake layer; top with second cake layer. Frost top of cake with remaining frosting; sprinkle with ¼ cup pecans.

TIPS *If using nut grater, grate approximately 1 cup toasted pecan halves and measure 1 cup. If using food processor, pulse scant 1 cup toasted pecan halves with 1 tablespoon of the flour until finely ground; measure 1 cup.

**To toast pecans, place on baking sheet; bake at 350°F. for 6 to 8 minutes or until slightly darker in color. Cool.

12 servings

PER SERVING: 555 calories, 29.5 g total fat (14 g saturated fat), 4.5 g protein, 71 g carbohydrate, 125 mg cholesterol, 190 mg sodium, 1.5 g fiber

RECIPE BY LISA SALTZMAN

Cinnamon-Apple Cake

Reminiscent of an old-fashioned plum pudding, this moist cake is bursting with cinnamon and apple flavor. It's served with a decadent hard sauce spiked with Grand Marnier. Sprinkle the cake with powdered sugar, if desired.

CAKE
- ¾ cup unsalted butter, melted
- 1½ cups sugar
- ½ cup packed brown sugar
- 2 eggs
- 2 cups all-purpose flour
- 1 tablespoon ground cinnamon
- 2 teaspoons baking soda
- 1 teaspoon salt
- 2 Fuji or Braeburn apples (1 lb.), peeled, chopped (3½ cups)
- 1 cup chopped walnuts
- 1 cup dried cranberries

SAUCE
- ½ cup unsalted butter, softened
- 1 cup powdered sugar
- 1 tablespoon orange-flavored liqueur, such as Grand Marnier or orange juice
- 1 tablespoon milk
- 2 teaspoons ground cinnamon
- ⅛ teaspoon salt

1 Heat oven to 325°F. Grease and flour 10-cup Bundt or tube pan.

2 Whisk melted butter, sugar and brown sugar in large bowl; whisk in eggs. Whisk flour, 1 tablespoon cinnamon, baking soda and 1 teaspoon salt in medium bowl; gently stir into butter mixture. Fold in apples, walnuts and cranberries. (Batter will be stiff.) Spoon into pan.

3 Bake 1 hour 5 minutes to 1 hour 15 minutes or until skewer inserted in center comes out clean. Cool on wire rack 15 minutes. Invert cake onto wire rack. Serve warm or at room temperature.*

4 Meanwhile, beat ½ cup butter and powdered sugar in medium bowl at medium-high speed 2 to 3 minutes or until well-blended. Add all remaining sauce ingredients; beat 1 minute or until smooth. Serve at room temperature. (Sauce can be made 2 days ahead. Cover and refrigerate.)

TIP *To warm cake, cover loosely with foil. Bake at 300°F. for 15 to 20 minutes.

12 servings

PER SERVING: 540 calories, 27 g total fat (13 g saturated fat), 5 g protein, 73.5 g carbohydrate, 85 mg cholesterol, 500 mg sodium, 2.5 g fiber

RECIPE BY LISA SALTZMAN

Spiced Peach-Pecan Upside-Down Cake

The perfect dessert for late summer, this gooey cake showcases juicy fresh peaches and chunky chopped pecans. A trio of baking spices laces it with warm, homey flavor.

10	tablespoons unsalted butter, softened, divided
⅔	cup packed light brown sugar
1	tablespoon lemon juice
12	oz. peaches (1 to 2 peaches), peeled, sliced (½ inch)*
½	cup chopped pecans
1	cup all-purpose flour
¾	teaspoon baking powder
½	teaspoon ground cinnamon
½	teaspoon ground nutmeg
¼	teaspoon ground cloves
¼	teaspoon salt
¾	cup sugar
1	teaspoon grated lemon peel
2	eggs
1	teaspoon vanilla extract
¼	cup peach nectar

1 Heat oven to 350°F. Spray sides of 9×2-inch round pan with nonstick cooking spray. Melt 4 tablespoons of the butter and brown sugar in medium saucepan over medium heat, stirring until sugar is dissolved and mixture is smooth and bubbly, about 5 minutes. Stir in lemon juice. Pour syrup into pan. Arrange peach slices over syrup; sprinkle with pecans.

2 In medium bowl, whisk together flour, baking powder, cinnamon, nutmeg, cloves and salt. In large bowl, beat remaining 6 tablespoons butter, sugar and lemon peel at medium speed 3 minutes or until light and fluffy. At low speed, beat in eggs one at a time, beating until blended. Beat in vanilla. Beat in flour mixture alternately with peach nectar, beginning and ending with flour mixture. Spoon and spread batter over peaches to cover completely.

3 Bake 35 to 45 minutes or until toothpick inserted in center comes out clean. Cool on wire rack 10 minutes. Run knife around edge to loosen cake. Place rimmed serving plate on top of cake. With oven mitts, carefully invert cake onto plate, holding pan upside-down about 15 seconds. Remove pan from cake. Serve warm or at room temperature.

TIP *To peel peaches, drop into large pot of boiling water; boil 30 seconds or until peach skins loosen. Remove with slotted spoon; drop into ice water to cool. Use knife to peel away skins.

8 servings

PER SERVING: 415 calories, 21 g total fat (10 g saturated fat), 4.5 g protein, 54.5 g carbohydrate, 90 mg cholesterol, 145 mg sodium, 2 g fiber

RECIPE BY MELANIE BARNARD

Chocolate Chip Cupcakes
with Cream Cheese Frosting

Chocolate Chip Cupcakes with Cream Cheese Frosting

These moist cupcakes are loaded with chocolate chips, ensuring a chocolate jolt in every bite. A hint of almond rounds out the flavor.

CUPCAKES

1¼	cups all-purpose flour
1	teaspoon baking powder
⅛	teaspoon salt
1	cup sugar
½	cup unsalted butter, softened
2	eggs
1	teaspoon vanilla extract
½	cup whole milk
1	cup miniature semisweet chocolate chips

FROSTING

3	oz. cream cheese, softened
2	tablespoons unsalted butter, softened
½	teaspoon vanilla extract
⅛	teaspoon almond extract
1¼	cups powdered sugar
¼	cup semisweet miniature chocolate chips

1 Heat oven to 350°F. Line 12 muffin cups with paper liners. In medium bowl, whisk together flour, baking powder and salt.

2 In large bowl, beat sugar and ½ cup butter at medium speed 2 minutes or until smooth and creamy. Add eggs one at a time, beating well after each addition. Beat in 1 teaspoon vanilla. At low speed, alternately beat in flour mixture with milk until incorporated, beginning and ending with flour mixture. Stir in 1 cup chocolate chips. Fill paper liners about three-fourths full with batter.

3 Bake 23 to 28 minutes or until toothpick inserted in center comes out with just a few crumbs attached. (If toothpick penetrates chocolate chip, test another spot.) Cool in pan on wire rack 15 minutes. Remove from pan; cool completely.

4 In large bowl, beat cream cheese and 2 tablespoons butter at medium speed until blended and smooth. Beat in ½ teaspoon vanilla and almond extract. At low speed, beat in powdered sugar until blended and smooth. Spread cupcakes with frosting; sprinkle with ¼ cup chocolate chips.

12 cupcakes

PER CUPCAKE: 375 calories, 18.5 g total fat (11 g saturated fat), 4 g protein, 51 g carbohydrate, 70 mg cholesterol, 105 mg sodium, 1.5 g fiber

RECIPE BY ELINOR KLIVANS

Creamy Chocolate-Malt Cake

Malt flavor infuses the crust, filling and topping of this luscious cake. Use chocolate stout in the mousse, if possible. It's a natural partner with semisweet chocolate.

CRUST
- 1¼ cups chocolate cookie crumbs*
- 1 cup crushed malted milk balls
- ¼ cup unsalted butter, melted

MOUSSE
- 12 oz. semisweet chocolate, chopped
- ⅔ cup chocolate stout or porter beer, or cold coffee
- 1½ teaspoons vanilla extract
- 1½ cups heavy whipping cream
- ¼ cup powdered sugar

GARNISH
- ½ cup heavy whipping cream
- 1 tablespoon powdered sugar
- 16 malted milk balls, coarsely crushed

1 In medium bowl, stir together cookie crumbs and 1 cup crushed malted milk balls. Stir in butter until well-blended. Press into bottom and 1½ inches up sides of 9-inch springform pan. Refrigerate.

2 Place semisweet chocolate and stout in medium microwave-safe bowl. Microwave on medium 1½ to 2 minutes; stir until chocolate is melted and smooth. (If necessary, continue microwaving chocolate mixture in 15-second increments, stirring after each interval, until chocolate is melted and smooth.) Stir in vanilla. Cool 5 to 10 minutes or until chocolate is no longer warm, stirring occasionally.

3 In large bowl, beat 1½ cups cream and ¼ cup powdered sugar at medium-high speed until soft peaks form. Stir ½ cup of the whipped cream into chocolate mixture; pour chocolate mixture into bowl with remaining whipped cream. Fold into whipped cream until well-blended; pour into crust. Cover and refrigerate several hours or until set. (Cake can be made to this point up to 1 day ahead.)

4 Just before serving, in medium bowl, beat ½ cup cream at medium-high speed until firm but not stiff peaks form. Stir in 1 tablespoon powdered sugar. Pipe or spoon into 12 mounds around top edge of cake; sprinkle with 16 crushed malted milk balls. Store in refrigerator.

TIP *Look for 100-percent chocolate cookie crumbs, such as the Oreo brand, which are located in the supermarket baking section near graham cracker crumbs or in the ice cream topping section. Do not use Oreo Crunchies, which are broken Oreo cookies that also contain the creme filling. If you can't find chocolate cookies in crumb form, purchase chocolate wafer cookies (such as the Famous brand) and crush them into fine crumbs.

12 servings

PER SERVING: 510 calories, 34 g total fat (22 g saturated fat), 4 g protein, 50.5 g carbohydrate, 65 mg cholesterol, 160 mg sodium, 3 g fiber

RECIPE BY MARY EVANS

Creamy Chocolate-Malt Cake

Pumpkin-Praline Cheesecake

Pumpkin-Praline Cheesecake

A crunchy praline-like topping is the perfect foil for this soft, creamy cheesecake. The rich pumpkin filling is scented with all the right spices, just like your favorite pumpkin pie.

CRUST

1	cup graham cracker crumbs
¼	cup unsalted butter, melted
1	tablespoon packed brown sugar
½	cup finely chopped toasted pecans*

TOPPING

½	cup packed brown sugar
½	cup whipping cream
¾	cup coarsely chopped toasted pecans*

CHEESECAKE

3	(8-oz.) pkg. cream cheese, softened
1	cup canned pure pumpkin
1	cup packed brown sugar
1½	teaspoons ground cinnamon
¾	teaspoon ground ginger
½	teaspoon ground cloves
4	eggs
1	tablespoon dark rum, if desired

1 Wrap bottom and sides of 9-inch springform pan with heavy-duty foil. In medium bowl, stir together all crust ingredients except pecans; press into bottom of pan. Sprinkle ½ cup pecans over crust. Refrigerate while preparing filling.

2 Heat oven to 300°F. Place cream cheese in food processor; process until smooth and creamy. Add pumpkin, 1 cup brown sugar, cinnamon, ginger and cloves; pulse to combine. Add eggs two at a time; pulse until well-blended. Add rum; pulse to combine. (Cheesecake also can be made with electric mixer.) Pour into pan.

3 Place springform pan in large shallow roasting or broiler pan. Fill pan with enough hot water to come halfway up sides of springform pan. Bake 65 to 75 minutes or until edges are puffed and top is dry to the touch. Center should move slightly when pan is tapped but should not ripple as if liquid. Remove cake from water bath; remove foil. Cool on wire rack 1 hour. Refrigerate at least 8 hours or overnight.

4 Place ½ cup brown sugar and cream in small saucepan; heat over medium heat until sugar dissolves, stirring frequently. Reduce heat to medium-low; simmer 5 minutes or until thickened (you should be able to see bottom of pan when stirring). (Topping will thicken more as it cools.)

5 Remove from heat; stir in ¾ cup pecans. Let stand until cool, 10 to 15 minutes. Pour over cheesecake, spreading with spatula. Refrigerate at least 30 minutes or until set. Store in refrigerator.

TIP *To toast pecans, place on baking sheet; bake at 350°F. for 6 to 8 minutes or until slightly darker in color. Cool.

12 servings

PER SERVING: 510 calories, 37.5 g total fat (18.5 g saturated fat), 8 g protein, 39 g carbohydrate, 155 mg cholesterol, 245 mg sodium, 2 g fiber

RECIPE BY LISA SALTZMAN

Brownie Chunk Cheesecake

Brownie Chunk Cheesecake

To get an idea of life member Ann Marie Otis' passion, look no further than her nickname, "the cake lady." "I started creating cheesecakes several years ago," she says. "It turned into a small business that I ran out of my house." After making hundreds of cheesecakes, what has she learned? "I finally decided that the cracks on top of the cake add character," she says.

CRUST

31	creme-filled chocolate cookies, crushed
¼	cup unsalted butter, melted

FILLING

3	(8-oz.) pkg. cream cheese, softened
1	cup sugar
1	tablespoon vanilla extract
1	cup sour cream
1	cup heavy whipping cream
4	eggs
¼	cup all-purpose flour
1½	cups coarsely chopped brownies

TOPPING

8	oz. milk chocolate, chopped
⅓	cup heavy whipping cream
2	oz. white chocolate, melted

1 Heat oven to 325°F. In medium bowl, stir together all crust ingredients. Press into bottom and 1 inch up sides of 9-inch springform pan. Wrap pan with heavy-duty foil; freeze 30 minutes.

2 In large bowl, beat cream cheese, sugar and vanilla at medium speed until blended. Beat in sour cream and 1 cup cream. Add eggs one at a time, beating just until blended. Slowly beat in flour. Fold in brownies.

3 Place springform pan in large baking or broiler pan. Pour batter into crust (batter will come to within ¼ inch of top edge). Add enough hot tap water to baking pan to come halfway up sides of springform pan. Bake 1 hour 15 minutes to 1 hour 30 minutes or until edges are puffed and top is dry to the touch. Center should move slightly when pan is tapped but should not ripple as if liquid.

4 Remove springform pan from baking pan; remove foil. Cool completely on wire rack. Refrigerate overnight.

5 Melt milk chocolate and ⅓ cup cream in medium saucepan over low heat, stirring until smooth. Pour over top of cheesecake; let stand 10 minutes.

6 Pour white chocolate into small resealable plastic bag; snip off corner of bag. Drizzle chocolate over cheesecake. Refrigerate at least 1 hour. Refrigerate leftovers.

12 servings

PER SERVING: 780 calories, 54.5 g total fat (29.5 g saturated fat), 12 g protein, 64 g carbohydrate, 205 mg cholesterol, 400 mg sodium, 2.5 g fiber

RECIPE BY LIFE MEMBER ANN MARIE OTIS, FAYETTEVILLE, NY

Cream Cheese-Apple Crisp

To create this apple-rich dessert, Member Sharon Rosen enhanced a basic crisp recipe by giving it a crust to make it easier to eat. She then added a layer of cream cheese to provide more body. When choosing apples, select those that hold their shape well, such as Golden Delicious or Jonagold.

TOPPING

- 1½ cups quick-cooking oatmeal
- 1⅓ cups all-purpose flour
- 1 cup packed brown sugar
- 2 teaspoons ground cinnamon
- ¾ cup butter, chilled, cut up

APPLES

- 6 cups peeled chopped apples (½ inch) (4 large apples)
- ⅓ cup sugar
- 2 tablespoons all-purpose flour
- 1 teaspoon ground cinnamon
- ¼ teaspoon salt

FILLING

- 1 (8-oz.) pkg. cream cheese, softened
- ½ cup sugar
- 2 eggs
- 2 tablespoons all-purpose flour
- 2 tablespoons milk

1 Heat oven to 350°F. In large bowl, stir together oatmeal, 1⅓ cups flour, brown sugar and 2 teaspoons cinnamon. Cut in butter until mixture is crumbly. Press half the mixture into bottom of 13×9-inch glass baking dish; reserve remaining mixture for topping.

2 In large bowl, toss together all apple ingredients until apples are coated. Spread over crust.

3 In large bowl, beat cream cheese and ½ cup sugar at medium speed until smooth. Add eggs, 2 tablespoons flour and milk; beat until combined. Spread over apple mixture; sprinkle with reserved oatmeal mixture.

4 Bake 40 to 45 minutes or until golden brown and apples are tender. Cool on wire rack.

12 servings

PER SERVING: 440 calories, 20 g total fat (10.5 g saturated fat), 6 g protein, 61.5 g carbohydrate, 85 mg cholesterol, 200 mg sodium, 3 g fiber

RECIPE BY MEMBER SHARON ROSEN, WELCOME, MN

Cream Cheese-Apple Crisp

Mixed Berry Cobbler

This cobbler is the perfect addition to your arsenal of summer dessert recipes because it's quick to fix and showcases fresh berries. If desired, top it with ice cream or whipped cream.

FILLING

6	cups fresh or frozen (unthawed) mixed berries (blueberries, blackberries, raspberries and/or strawberries)
¾	cup sweet fruit wine, such as blackberry or cherry
2	teaspoons vanilla extract
¾	cup sugar
3	tablespoons quick-cooking tapioca
1	teaspoon ground cinnamon

TOPPING

1¾	cups old-fashioned rolled oats
1	cup all-purpose flour
¾	cup packed brown sugar
¾	cup chopped toasted walnuts or pecans*
¾	cup butter, melted
2	teaspoons vanilla extract
1½	teaspoons ground cinnamon

1 Heat oven to 350°F. Place berries in 8-inch square baking dish; add wine and vanilla. Sprinkle with sugar, tapioca and cinnamon (no need to stir).

2 In large bowl, stir together all topping ingredients; sprinkle over fruit. Pat down gently.

3 Bake 1 hour or until top is golden brown and juices are bubbling. Serve warm or at room temperature.

TIP *To toast walnuts, place on baking sheet; bake at 350°F. for 6 to 8 minutes or until pale brown and fragrant. Cool.

8 servings

PER SERVING: 575 calories, 26 g total fat (12 g saturated fat), 7.5 g protein, 80.5 g carbohydrate, 45 mg cholesterol, 135 mg sodium, 7 g fiber

RECIPE BY MEMBER BOBBIE ARENTZOFF, THOUSAND OAKS, CA

Mixed Berry Cobbler

Oatmeal-Cherry Cookies, page 135
Ginger-Molasses Cookies, page 136

Oatmeal-Cherry Cookies

You'll love biting into these wonderfully soft cookies that are dressed up with walnuts and sweet dried cherries. For a variation of these soft cookies, substitute another dried fruit, such as cranberries or apricots.

1	cup unsalted butter, melted, cooled
1	cup packed dark brown sugar
⅔	cup sugar
2	eggs
1	teaspoon vanilla extract
1½	cups all-purpose flour
2	teaspoons baking powder
½	teaspoon salt
3	cups old-fashioned rolled oats
1½	cups dried cherries
1	cup coarsely chopped walnuts

1 Heat oven to 375°F. Line 3 to 4 baking sheets with parchment paper.

2 In large bowl, whisk together melted butter, brown sugar and sugar. Whisk in eggs and vanilla until well-blended. In medium bowl, whisk together flour, baking powder and salt. Stir into butter mixture. Stir in all remaining ingredients.

3 Use #16 cookie scoop or ¼ cup measure to scoop dough; place on baking sheets, leaving at least 3 inches between cookies. Flatten gently into 3-inch rounds.

4 Bake 12 to 15 minutes or until light golden brown around edges but still pale in center and slightly soft. Remove from oven; immediately slide parchment paper onto wire racks to cool.

24 (4-inch) cookies

PER COOKIE: 255 calories, 12 g total fat (5.5 g saturated fat), 4 g protein, 34.5 g carbohydrate, 40 mg cholesterol, 100 mg sodium, 2.5 g fiber

RECIPE BY LISA SALTZMAN

Ginger-Molasses Cookies

A quartet of spices livens up these dark, rich cookies. They get additional depth of flavor from molasses and a nice kick from crystallized ginger. They're perfect for true spice lovers.

- ¾ cup unsalted butter, melted, cooled
- ¾ cup packed dark brown sugar
- 1 egg
- ¾ cup mild molasses
- 3 cups all-purpose flour
- 2 teaspoons ground ginger
- 2 teaspoons ground cinnamon
- 1 teaspoon ground nutmeg
- 1 teaspoon ground cloves
- 1 teaspoon baking soda
- ½ teaspoon salt
- ¼ cup sugar
- 2 tablespoons coarsely chopped crystallized ginger

1 Heat oven to 375°F. Line 3 baking sheets with parchment paper.

2 In medium bowl, whisk together melted butter and brown sugar. Whisk in egg and molasses until well-blended. In another medium bowl, whisk together all remaining ingredients except sugar and crystallized ginger. Stir into butter mixture. Cover and refrigerate at least 1 hour.

3 Meanwhile, place sugar and crystallized ginger in food processor; pulse until finely ground. Pour into small bowl.

4 Working with one-third of the dough at a time (keep remaining dough refrigerated), use #16 cookie scoop or ¼ cup measure to scoop dough. Roll into 1¾-inch balls. Lightly roll and press each ball in crystallized ginger mixture; place on baking sheets, leaving about 3 inches between cookies. Gently flatten into 2¼-inch rounds.

5 Bake 12 to 15 minutes or until just golden brown around edges but still slightly soft. Remove from oven; immediately slide parchment paper onto wire racks to cool.

18 (4-inch) cookies

PER COOKIE: 240 calories, 8.5 g total fat (5 g saturated fat), 2.5 g protein, 39.5 g carbohydrate, 30 mg cholesterol, 150 mg sodium, 1 g fiber

RECIPE BY LISA SALTZMAN

What Makes Cookies Soft and Chewy?

Melt the Butter

Most cookie recipes call for creaming softened butter and sugar. This process beats air into the batter, resulting in light-textured, tender cookies. But to produce chewy, thick cookies, it's best if you use melted butter. It coats the flour more thoroughly, creating a denser texture and a chewiness similar to a brownie or bar cookie.

Use Brown Sugar

The type of sugar used in cookies directly affects their flavor and texture. White sugar has a low moisture content, creating a crisp cookie. Brown sugar contains molasses and is more moist, resulting in softer cookies that stay soft, even after baking. Oatmeal-Cherry Cookies (pg. 135) use a combination of white and brown sugar, while Ginger-Molasses Cookies (pg. 136) use only brown sugar.

Don't Overbake

Remove cookies from the oven when they're slightly underdone. They should just start to brown around the edges and still be slightly puffy. They should be a pale golden brown, not a rich brown. Check the cookies when they've baked the minimum amount of time as stated in the recipe; then watch them closely. If you're not sure if they're done, use a spatula and peek at the underside of a cookie to check its color. It should be pale brown.

Useful Tools

If you enjoy making cookies, invest in some equipment that will help ensure success.

A Cookie Scoop

To make sure cookies bake evenly on a baking sheet, you need to have uniformly sized balls of dough. You can use a measuring cup, but an easier way is to use a cookie scoop (about $10). The best ones work like an ice cream scoop. Dip the scoop into the dough and drop the dough onto the baking sheet by squeezing the handle. If the scoop starts to gum up as you work, just dip it in granulated sugar between scoops.

Baking Sheet Liners

Lining baking sheets makes it easier to remove the baked cookies and to clean up afterward. We use parchment paper in these recipes, but you also can use a silicone baking mat. Neither requires greasing.

Grand German Chocolate Bars

Grand German Chocolate Bars

Shortbread provides a buttery base for these towering, fudgy bars. The rich chocolate layer is flecked with coconut and pecans and crowned with a gooey coconut-pecan topping.

CRUST
- 1 cup all-purpose flour
- ½ cup packed light brown sugar
- ½ cup sweetened flaked coconut
- 6 tablespoons unsalted butter, cut up, softened

BARS
- 6 oz. semisweet chocolate, chopped
- 6 tablespoons unsalted butter, softened
- 1 cup all-purpose flour
- ½ teaspoon salt
- 2 eggs
- 1 cup packed light brown sugar
- 1 teaspoon vanilla extract
- 1½ cups sweetened flaked coconut
- 1½ cups chopped toasted pecans*

TOPPING
- ½ cup heavy whipping cream
- ½ cup sugar
- 1 egg
- 1 tablespoon unsalted butter, softened
- 1½ cups sweetened flaked coconut
- 1½ cups chopped toasted pecans*
- 1 teaspoon vanilla extract

1 Heat oven to 350°F. Line 8-inch square pan with heavy-duty foil, leaving extra foil extending over edges. Spray with nonstick cooking spray.

2 In medium bowl, with fork, mix together all crust ingredients until crumbly; press into pan. Bake 5 minutes.

3 Meanwhile, place chocolate and 6 tablespoons butter in medium heatproof bowl; place over medium saucepan of barely simmering water. Stir frequently until mixture is melted and smooth. Remove bowl from saucepan; let stand until cooled slightly.

4 In small bowl, stir together 1 cup flour and salt. In large bowl, beat 2 eggs and 1 cup brown sugar at medium speed 1 minute or until well-blended and lightened in color. At low speed, beat in chocolate mixture and 1 teaspoon vanilla until blended. Add flour mixture, beating just until incorporated. Stir in 1½ cups coconut and 1½ cups pecans. Spread batter over crust.

5 Bake 35 to 45 minutes or until toothpick inserted 2 inches from edge comes out with moist crumbs attached (toothpick inserted in center comes out with thin fudge coating). Top of bars may crack around edges. Cool completely on wire rack. (Bars may sink slightly during cooking.)

6 In medium saucepan, whisk together cream, sugar, 1 egg and 1 tablespoon butter. Cook over medium heat until bubbles form around outside edge, stirring constantly. Reduce heat to low; cook 1 to 2 minutes or until thickened. Stir in 1½ cups coconut, 1½ cups pecans and 1 teaspoon vanilla. Spread over cooled bars. Cool completely.

7 Using foil edges, lift bars from pan. Slide bars off foil onto cutting board; cut into 16 pieces. (Bars can be made up to 2 days ahead. Cover and store at room temperature.)

TIP *To toast pecans, place on baking sheet; bake at 350°F. for 6 to 8 minutes or until slightly darker in color. Cool.

16 bars

PER BAR: 555 calories, 37 g total fat (16 g saturated fat), 6 g protein, 56 g carbohydrate, 75 mg cholesterol, 140 mg sodium, 4 g fiber

RECIPE BY ELINOR KLIVANS

Cranberry-Date Streusel Bars

Cranberry-Date Streusel Bars

Some people, like life member Ginny O'Brien, are just born to bake. "My great-grandfather was a master baker in Germany," she says, "and I've inherited his baking genes." For years she's been using her great-grandfather's recipes to make large batches of cookies at Christmas. Ginny decided to add a bar cookie to round out the selection and did a bit of research to come up with the basic recipe. She looked to her pantry to create the fruit filling, and a soon-to-be classic was born.

BARS

1	cup packed brown sugar
¾	cup butter, softened
1¾	cups all-purpose flour
½	teaspoon baking soda
½	teaspoon salt
1½	cups quick-cooking oats

FILLING

1½	cups chopped dates
¼	cup sugar
1½	cups raisins
½	cup dried cranberries
½	cup chopped walnuts, toasted*

1 Heat oven to 400°F. Beat sugar and butter in medium bowl at medium speed 2 to 3 minutes or until thoroughly blended. Combine flour, baking soda and salt in medium bowl; slowly beat into butter mixture. Beat in oats. Press half of the mixture into bottom of 13×9-inch baking pan.

2 Place dates and sugar in medium saucepan; barely cover with water. Bring to a boil; boil 10 minutes or until thickened. Stir in raisins, cranberries and walnuts. Cool.

3 Gently spread filling over crust; sprinkle with remaining crust mixture. Bake 20 to 30 minutes or until golden brown. Cool on wire rack 30 minutes. Cut into bars while slightly warm. (Bars can be made 3 days ahead.)

TIP *To toast walnuts, place on baking sheet; bake at 400°F. for 3 to 5 minutes or until pale brown and fragrant. Cool.

24 bars

PER BAR: 230 calories, 8 g total fat (4 g saturated fat), 2.5 g protein, 39.5 g carbohydrate, 15 mg cholesterol, 120 mg sodium, 2.5 g fiber

RECIPE BY LIFE MEMBER GINNY O'BRIEN, WEST DOVER, VT

Recipe Index

General Index